art of the Slow Cooker

art of the Slow Cooker

80 EXCITING NEW RECIPES

By Andrew Schloss

Photographs by Yvonne Duivenvoorden

CHRONICLE BOOKS
SAN FRANCISCO

Library of Congress Cataloging-in-Publication Data

Schloss, Andrew, 1951-

  Art of the slow cooker : 80 exciting new recipes / Andrew Schloss ; photographs by Yvonne Duivenvoorden.

    p. cm.

  Includes index.

  ISBN 978-0-8118-5912-7 (alk. paper)

  1. Electric cookery, Slow. I. Title.

  TX827.S35 2008

  641.5'884--dc22

                    2007042021

ISBN 978-0-8118-5912-7

Manufactured in China.

Prop styling Catherine Doherty

Food styling by Lucie Richard, www.lucierichard.ca

Studio production by Raff Melito, www.fullserveproductions.com

Designed by Anne Donnard

Typesetting by DC Typography

The photographer wishes to thank the aforementioned team of very talented women who helped to make this project so enjoyable and, above all, memorable. Well done, ladies!!

10 9 8 7

Chronicle Books LLC

680 Second Street

San Francisco, California 94107

www.chroniclebooks.com

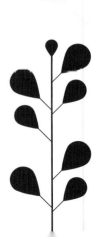

Dedication

To Karen, my compass.

THANK YOU

To Yvonne Duivenvoorden, an extraordinary food photographer, who orchestrated the sumptuous photos that grace these pages, along with prop stylist Catherine Doherty and food stylist Lucie Richard.

To everyone at Chronicle who devoted their creativity and intelligence to build this book: production coordinator, Ben Kasman; book designer, Anne Donnard; for marketing, Peter Perez; and Amy Portello for publicity. And special thanks to my editor and friend, Bill LcBlond, a gentleman whose impeccable taste and steady judgment can make even an author like me look good, and to Amy Treadwell, who coordinates everything for everyone.

To Lisa Ekus, my book agent, and the best friend an isolated lonely author could have.

To everyone who kindly tested and tasted the many failures you have to go through to get to a handful of successes that are worth publishing: Tara Mataraza Desmond, Carol Moore, Phil Schulman, Debby and Ned Carroll, Debra Shain, and Murry Silberman. And, of course, to my family: Karen, Dana, Ben, and Isaac Schloss, whose critiques continue to make me a better cook.

To Judith Finlayson, my slow cooker mentor for indispensable council and advice.

To David Joachim, my sometimes co-author, for helping me reason through some thorny issues about slow cookers, and for offering perspectives that help me to be a kinder and smarter man than I would otherwise be.

Table of Contents

Introduction

BY MEASURING CULINARY EASE WITH A STOPWATCH, we forget that there are ways to cook, as old as fire itself, that take little work and even less attention as they infuse food with a goodness that only time can give. And all they require is that we slow down.

Slow-cooked food simmers and spits lazily while we play. It rests on a low setting while we rest in the next room. It simmers gently in a fragrant broth while we run errands, finish up work, or just have fun. And the best part is that while we're occupied elsewhere, ingredients are being transformed: flavors are blending, blossoming, and balancing. Sometimes the best thing a cook can do is sit back and wait.

I believe in ease. In fact, I have spent my career finding ways for home cooks to get dinner on the table with less work, in less time, and with better results. Though I am devoted to streamlining the effort expended in the kitchen, I recognize there is a danger in believing too much in ease. When making cooking easy becomes more important than making good food, we're all in trouble. And I fear that's what has happened to slow cooking.

When I told my friends I was working on a slow cooker book, all their responses were nearly identical: "I love my slow cooker. I just throw everything in it and walk away." Not so fast. I don't know of any cooking technique that benefits from complete neglect. Roasting doesn't take a lot of attention, but if you don't season the roast well, check the internal temperature for doneness, and baste every now and then, you are liable to end up with a large joint of jerky.

Slow cooking has many advantages, the main one being that the heat is so gentle, you can simmer dinner for hours without worrying about overcooking it. And there are some dishes, like the classic Barbecued Baked Beans (page 154), Slow-Cooked South Carolina Pulled Pork (page 95), or All-Day Cassoulet (page 135), that I wouldn't do any other way. A slow cooker turns tough, gnarly cuts of meat into succulent, melt-in-your-mouth feasts, but it won't brown a brisket or roast a chicken. Slow cooking is easy, but it's not effortless, and the more you take heed of both its strengths and its limitations, the more artful your efforts will be.

The Art of Slow Cooking

SLOW COOKERS CONSIST OF THREE PARTS: (1) a metal casing, which contains an electric heating element and heat controls; (2) a ceramic insert, or crock, which fits inside the metal casing; and (3) a lid. (For more details, see Choosing a Slow Cooker, page 12.) The main benefit of slow cooking derives from the heating properties of ceramic. The material heats up slowly and gives off heat gradually. Provided that the heat source is steady and controlled, a ceramic pot can warm food to a set temperature and keep it there for hours without fear of scorching or overheating.

On the other hand, ceramic pots are terrible for browning or searing. In cooking, brown is not just a color. It is a flavor—the flavor of succulence, which is why most of my slow cooker recipes start by browning ingredients in a skillet. During browning, sugars and proteins on the surface of meats and vegetables caramelize, transforming into hundreds of highly charged aromatic flavor components.

This is why we make a bad trade-off when we see slow cooking as merely a dump-and-heat cooking method. You may get something hot for dinner, but that's about it. I say take a little more time, dirty another pan, and create food that will not just fill the belly, but delight the senses as well.

This initial cooking step outside of the slow cooker releases the fat-soluble aromatics in onions and garlic, as well as the scents of herbs and spices, and gives them a head start in the cooking process. The hard fibers of root vegetables soften, which helps them to cook more evenly, giving you a chance to perfect a sauce.

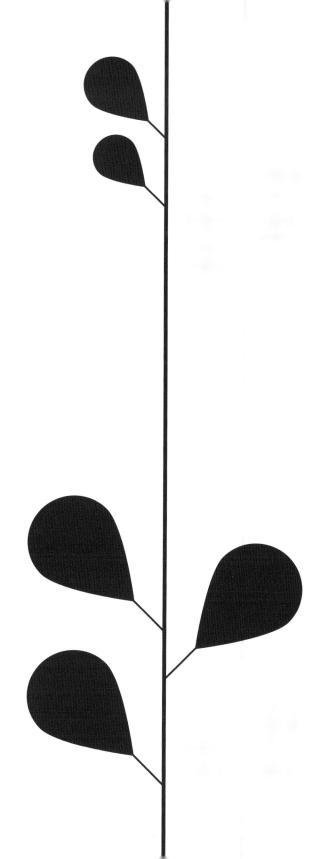

choosing a slow cooker

Although all slow cookers operate similarly, there are differences, more often between models than between brands. When choosing a slow cooker, you will need to consider:

- **SIZE** Slow cookers range in size from 1 to 8 quarts, although most are between 3 and 6 quarts. If you have a large family or like to plan on leftovers, you will want a large cooker of at least 5 quarts. Smaller models, between 3 and 4 quarts, will make fewer portions (no more than 6), or they will hold a dip for a crowd. Most people who use their slow cookers frequently have both a large and a small model. You should always use a slow cooker that fits the amount of food you are cooking. For best results, the crock should be at least one-third, but no more than three-quarters, full.

- **SHAPE** Small slow cookers are usually round, and large cookers are usually oval. Given those basics, there can be countless differences in dimensions, which don't matter much unless you are planning to bake in your slow cooker. In that case you will need a slow cooker with a minimum interior width of 7 inches to accommodate a medium baking pan. You will also find many specialty slow cooker shapes: shallow rectangles for casseroles, football-shaped ones for Super Bowl, basketball spheroids for March Madness, and filigreed gravy boat–shaped slow cookers that can be brought to the table.

- **CONTROLS** Basic slow cookers have three settings: low (heats between 185°F and 200°F), high (heats between 250°F and 300°F), and off. Many models also have a warm setting, which holds the contents at about 165°F. Most manufacturers recommend not holding food on warm for more than 2 hours. I have used the warm setting for up to 6 hours, however, without any problems. None of these conventional cookers keep track of time; once you set them up and turn them on, they stay at one setting until they are manually turned off or switched to warm, which is preferable to holding food at low. Several years ago, programmable slow cookers were introduced; these automatically switch to warm at a set time. The early versions have four time settings: 4 or 6 hours on high, and 8 or 10 hours on low. Now several brands of programmable slow cookers allow you to set the timing by half-hour or minute increments (from 1 minute to 20 hours). At the set time, they will switch to warm, but they cannot switch from high to low or switch off automatically. These machines tend to cost three to four times more than nonprogrammable models.

- **HEATING** Although all slow cookers say that their low setting is 200°F and high is 300°F, the truth is that there is a wide range. To test how well your slow cooker heats, put 2 quarts of room temperature water in the cooker, cover, and turn to low. After 3 hours the water should be hotter than 140°F, and after 6 hours it should be at least 180°F. Older slow cookers will tend to top out on low at around 185°F, while newer ones will get slightly hotter than 200°F. If, after heating the water for 6 hours, your cooker is hotter than 205°F or lower than 180F°, adjust your cooking times accordingly. If it is much lower, buy a new cooker; the one you have is not heating fast enough to ensure that the food you are cooking is safe.

- **APPEARANCE** Slow cookers come in a variety of cases and finishes. You can get them in colors coordinated to your kitchen, decorated with a country motif, clad in stainless steel, or emblazoned with a NASCAR collage—none of which has anything to do with performance.

- **BRANDS** There are more than a dozen major manufacturers of slow cookers, and most of them have several models, making the choices seem endless. In my experience, no brand is categorically better than another, and since they all introduce several new models every year, it is impossible to predict what the future will hold.

There is almost always a liquid ingredient in a slow cooker recipe. At some point, that liquid has to be turned into a sauce, a broth, or a glaze, or at least something more delicious than flavored water. There is much less evaporation from a slow cooker than there is from a saucepan or a skillet simmering on a stove top. For one thing, the heat of a slow cooker is quite low, so there is a minimal development of steam. And since slow cooking must be done covered, there's no place for the steam to go except to drip back into the pot.

The closed system of a slow cooker ensures that the heat remains constant and ingredients stay moist, but it also inhibits flavors from concentrating. One of the principal ways flavor develops in traditional cooking is through water evaporation. As the percentage of water reduces in a sauce, stew, or soup, the concentration of flavorful elements increases. At the same time, the percentage of solid particles increases, causing the liquid to thicken. In slow cooking neither process happens, so the only way to end up with intense, dynamic flavors and smooth, creamy textures is to make sure they're there before the slow cooker ever gets turned on.

Here's what you can do:

- Start with a minimum amount of liquid. As meats and vegetables simmer in a slow cooker, they release their juices into whatever liquid you already have in the recipe. That means that at the end of cooking, you will generally have about twice the amount of liquid you started with. For soups, you should start with about ½ cup of liquid per serving (remembering that the juices in the canned tomatoes, wine, or lemon juice you add for flavoring count as part of that liquid). For stews, start with about ¼ cup liquid per serving, and for sauces, about 2 tablespoons of liquid for each serving.

- Never use water. In slow cooking, water is the "antispice"—it sucks away flavor. So if you are going to add liquid, use broth, wine, juice, or something else that adds flavor.

- Season assertively (except for hot peppers). Have a free hand with salt and spices and try to use herbs as close to their whole form as possible. Whole herbs and spices release their flavors gradually. Preground spices tend to be less flavorful to begin with, and they will release most of their flavor during the first hour of cooking. Hot peppers (not peppercorns) have a tendency to take over during slow cooking. What seems like a pinch added at the start will grow into a painful punch after hours of simmering. For that reason, I usually add chiles near the end of cooking.

- Thicken cooking liquids before you add them to the slow cooker—about 50 percent thicker than you want them to be for serving. Although I use several different methods of thickening liquid in slow cooking, my standard is to coat meats with seasoned flour for browning, and reserve the remaining seasoned flour to thicken the liquid. I will usually use between ¼ cup and ⅓ cup flour for 6 servings, regardless of whether I am making a soup, stew, or sauce. Since the amount of liquid varies in each of these preparations, keeping the measurement of flour constant gives me just the right consistency for each type of recipe.

- Sometimes you may need to adjust the viscosity of a soup, stew, or sauce at the end of cooking. If it's too thick (I can't remember this ever happening), add a bit more broth, juice, or which- ever liquid (other than alcohol) was originally called for in the recipe. If it is too thin, add 1 or 2 tablespoons of instant mashed potato flakes. Although I would never ever serve instant mashed potatoes to anyone I love, I always keep a box on hand. It is the perfect fix for a thin soup, stew, or sauce, thickening the errant liquid instantly. The flakes never lump, and there is no residual potato flavor when used in such a small concentration. If you are making a glaze, in which a starch thickener would be inappropriate, the best course of action is to remove the solid ingre- dients from the cooker, pour the liquid into a skillet, and boil it over high heat until it thickens, which should happen in a few minutes.

Good and Slow

I AM DETERMINED to only give you recipes that deliver the best possible results from your slow cooker, but I am also aware that most slow cooker devotees are motivated more by the machine's ability to cook untended all day than by a quest for dynamic, high-quality recipes. I confess that meeting both of these criteria in every recipe has been a challenge. I have worked hard to create recipes that are as good as anything you could cook with a traditional cooking method, yet slow enough to simmer for at least 8 hours (the magic time frame for anyone with a day job). I cooked in more than a dozen styles of slow cookers and tried every recipe in these pages several times. Here's what I've discovered:

- Most meats reach an internal temperature of doneness within 4 hours, even on low, so letting them cook for another 4 hours overcooks them. The solution is to stop the cooking at 4 hours, which requires your presence, an expensive programmable slow cooker, or for you to only slow-cook meats that aren't ruined by extra cooking. For most recipes, I have chosen the latter. This means I generally do not slow-cook chicken breasts, beef fillets, pork chops, or any other cut of meat without sufficient internal fat and connective tissue to benefit from spending the better part of a day at a near-simmer. Fortunately, there are many candidates that give stellar results: any shoulder or chuck cut, brisket, short ribs, shanks, tri-tips, and flank steak. It is my belief that any meat lover will be able to find ample choices without resorting to endless repetition or ending up with a desiccated dinner.

- Although people often associate slow cooking with meats, the easiest, most foolproof ingredients for slow cooking are actually vegetables, particularly hard, fibrous root vegetables, such as beets, carrots, and sweet potatoes, which turn sweet and creamy in the crucible of a slow cooker. Soft or very moist vegetables, like spinach or zucchini, can be slow cooked, but they should be added in the last minutes. If you are cooking a combination of vegetables and meat, you can balance out the differences in their cooking times by layering fibrous vegetables on the bottom, meat in the middle, and tender, moist vegetables on top. Fresh vegetables may be cut up to 24 hours ahead and kept in the refrigerator until you are ready to cook them.

- Slow cookers produce meats and vegetables of unsurpassed tenderness, but after hours at a near simmer, the textures in slow-cooked foods can become homogenous. The remedy is to add fresh ingredients at the very end. A handful of chopped herbs, a jolt of peppers, a spark of grated citrus zest, or a crunch of toasted nuts can transform a long-cooking stew, a braised lamb shank, or a bread pudding into something extraordinary.

- I originally thought the slow cooker would be the perfect vehicle for getting more whole grains on the table, but after countless pots of gummy, sticky, exploded brown rice, wheat berries, quinoa, and teff (a fine grain), I gave up. There are a few grain dishes that benefit from the runny texture they get in a slow cooker, however. Barley risotto works well, and is far superior to risotto cooked in a slow cooker with traditional medium-grain rice. Grits were another winner. I found no easier way to make wonderful, creamy grits.

- The idea of using the slow cooker for baking intrigued me. In theory there is no reason it won't work. An oven is a box surrounded by heating elements that fire up the walls and floor, causing them to radiate heat and cook anything you place inside. The main difference is that a slow cooker is much smaller than a typical oven, and so you need to make allowances.

   First you need a baking pan that will fit in the cooker; my standard is a 1½-quart soufflé dish (with a diameter of less than 7 inches), which fits perfectly into most 6-quart, or larger, slow cookers. Next you have to do something to reduce the moisture in the cooker. Even if you don't add water to the cooker (which is often done to regulate the temperature directly around the baking dish), moisture coming from the cake or pudding will get trapped under the lid, causing the baked good to steam rather than bake. To absorb the extra moisture, place a folded flat-weave kitchen towel under the lid.

   With this modification, I have slow-cooked cheesecakes, fruitcakes, pudding cakes, crisps, and steamed puddings with great success. Quick breads and sponge cakes were less impressive, however. I recommend that you stick to moist, dense cakes. Slow cookers cannot produce a cake with a buttery crumb or an aerated texture.

slow cooking by ingredient

Slow cookers are almost always used to cook recipes that combine a variety of ingredients, so it is a bit difficult to talk about the specific needs of particular ingredients during slow cooking. Yet I always find it helpful to understand the affinities and tolerances of ingredients when figuring out how best to cook them.

The following table will give you an overview of how to slow-cook various ingredients, with the caveat that you will probably never cook any of them alone. As a result, recipes including these ingredients will probably reflect a compromise that accommodates the needs of all of the ingredients in the recipe.

INGREDIENTS	PREPARATION		SLOW COOK TIME	
	Cold Prep	Precook	High	Low
Apples, wedges	peeled	sautéed lightly	2–3 hrs.	4–6 hrs.
Apples, whole	peeled, cored	none	2–3 hrs.	4–6 hrs.
Apricots	halved, peeled	none	2 hrs.	4 hrs.
Artichoke, globe	trimmed	none	3–4 hrs.	NA
Artichoke, hearts	canned	none	2–4 hrs.	2–10 hrs.
Bananas	peeled, sliced	none	1–3 hrs.	2–6 hrs.
Barley	washed	none	3–4 hrs.	6–8 hrs.
Beans, canned	rinsed	none	2–6 hrs.	4–10 hrs.
Beans, dried	soaked	none	NA	8–12 hrs.
Beef, brisket	seasoned	browned	4–6 hrs.	8–10 hrs.
Beef, chuck	seasoned	browned	NA	8–10 hrs.
Beef, corned	seasoned	none	4–5 hrs.	8–10 hrs.
Beef, cubes	seasoned	browned	3–4 hrs.	6–8 hrs.
Beef, ground	seasoned	browned	3–4 hrs.	6–8 hrs.
Beef, oxtail	seasoned	browned	4–5 hrs.	8–10 hrs.
Beef, short ribs	seasoned	browned	3–4 hrs.	6–8 hrs.
Beef, sirloin	seasoned	browned	4–5 hrs.	8–9 hrs.
Beets	peeled, wedges	blanched	2–3 hrs.	4–5 hrs.
Carrots	chunks	sautéed	3–4 hrs.	4–10 hrs.
Cauliflower	cut into florets	none	2–3 hrs.	4–8 hrs.
Celery	sliced	sautéed	2–3 hrs.	2–8 hrs.
Chicken, dark	skinned	browned	3–4 hrs.	5–7 hrs.
Chicken, whole	halved or cut up	browned	3–4 hrs.	5–6 hrs.
Chiles	seeds removed	none	10 min.	NA
Corn kernels	none	none	2–4 hrs.	2–8 hrs.
Duck, whole	skinned, cut up	browned	2–3 hrs.	4–6 hrs.
Eggplant	cut into chunks	browned	3–4 hrs.	6–8 hrs.

INGREDIENTS	PREPARATION		SLOW COOK TIME	
	Cold Prep	Precook	High	Low
Fennel	sliced	browned	3–4 hrs.	6–8 hrs.
Fish	cut into chunks	none	20 min.	NA
Fish, large	filleted	browned	NA	2–3 hrs.
Lamb, cubes	seasoned	browned	3–4 hrs.	6–8 hrs.
Lamb, shanks	seasoned	browned	4–5 hrs.	6–8 hrs.
Lamb, shoulder	seasoned	browned	3–4 hrs.	6–8 hrs.
Leeks	thickly sliced	browned	2–3 hrs.	4–6 hrs.
Mushrooms	trimmed	browned	2–3 hrs.	4–8 hrs.
Onions	peeled, chopped	sautéed	2–3 hrs.	4–8 hrs.
Peaches	peeled, cut into wedges	none	2 hrs.	4 hrs.
Peppers, bell	trimmed, chopped	sautéed	2–3 hrs.	3–8 hrs.
Pork, country ribs	seasoned	browned	3–4 hrs.	6–8 hrs.
Pork, shoulder	seasoned	browned	3–4 hrs.	6–8 hrs.
Pork, sirloin	seasoned	browned	NA	6–8 hrs.
Potatoes	cubed	browned/none	3–4 hrs.	6–8 hrs.
Potatoes, sweet	peeled, cubed	browned/none	3–4 hrs.	6–8 hrs.
Shellfish, fresh	washed	none	20 min	NA
Spinach	stemmed	none	1–4 min	NA
Squash, summer	thickly sliced	none	30 min.	NA
Squash, winter	peeled, cut into chunks	none	3–4 hrs.	6–8 hrs.
Tomatoes, canned	diced	none	2–6 hrs.	4–10 hrs.
Tomatoes, fresh	diced	none	2–4 hrs.	4–8 hrs.
Turkey, legs	skinless	browned	3–4 hrs.	6–8 hrs.
Turnips	peeled, cut up	sautéed	3–4 hrs.	6–8 hrs.
Veal, cubes	seasoned	browned	3–4 hrs.	6–7 hrs.
Veal, shank	seasoned	browned	3–4 hrs.	6–8 hrs.

Slow and Safe

BACTERIA GROW MOST RAPIDLY at temperatures between 40°F (refrigerator temperature) and 140°F. The longer food stays in this danger zone, the greater the chance of a food safety issue, so it is important to get the contents of a slow cooker above 140°F as quickly as possible. So far I have only talked about precooking as a way to achieve better flavor and texture in the finished dish, but it is also the primary way to keep food safe. By adding hot food to a slow cooker you virtually eliminate any danger of bacterial growth. Here are some other ways you can keep your slow-cooked food safe:

- Do not brown or partially cook ingredients and refrigerate them. Always add browned ingredients directly to the cooker.

- When cooking a large cut of meat, such as corned beef, without browning it first, cook it on high for at least 1 hour to help it reach safe temperatures sooner.

- Keep raw food refrigerated until you cook it. Do not allow food to rest at room temperature beforehand.

- Do not start with frozen food.

- Try not to lift the lid during cooking. Every time the lid is removed, it takes about 20 minutes for the cooker to regain temperature.

- If you can't serve slow-cooked food within 2 hours of cooking, it should be refrigerated and reheated. Do not reheat food in a slow cooker. It will not get hot enough fast enough to ensure safety.

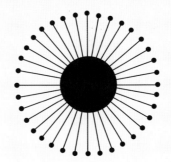

The Art of Homemade Soup

LONG AGO, IN A KITCHEN VERY MUCH LIKE YOURS, someone cooked for hours at a time. She kneaded bread and rolled out pastry, and whenever the winds blew cold, she whipped up a pot of soup. Now homemade soup is considered so time-consuming that most home cooks never try, but that is exactly why soups are a cinch in a slow cooker: it transforms the long hours of barely simmering ingredients into a convenience. Although almost any soup recipe can be adapted to slow cooking, bean soups, vegetable soups, pureed soups, and long-simmering meat soups make the most sense.

As with all slow cooker recipes, these soups start with less liquid than you would use in a soup pot on a stove top. For many of them the amount of liquid is not even enough to cover the solid ingredients. Don't add more; as the soup simmers, juices released from the vegetables and the bits of meat will enrich the broth deliciously.

Recipes

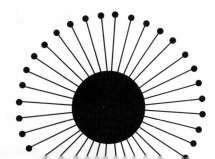

Chocolate Chicken Chili Soup

SWF (soup-weary forager) seeking something dark and sultry, your dream soup has arrived. This bitter-sweet chicken chili can be a simple, hearty, family-friendly meal one night and a provocative, spicy seduction the next. It's all a question of how you serve it. Try serving it with a side of cornbread and salad during the week, or scattering toasted hazelnuts on top and garnishing with freshly grated lemon zest for a romantic supper for two.

6

SERVINGS

PRECOOK

10 minutes

SLOW COOK

3 to 4 hours on high, or 6 to 8 hours on low, in a 5- to 6-quart slow cooker

AT THE END

2 minutes

2	tablespoons vegetable oil
2	pounds boneless chicken meat (dark and/or light), cut into ½-inch pieces
1	large onion, finely chopped
4	cloves garlic, minced
1	teaspoon ground cumin, preferably ground from whole seeds toasted in a dry skillet
1	teaspoon dried oregano
1	teaspoon dried thyme
2	teaspoons hot chili powder
½	teaspoon ground cinnamon
1	teaspoon kosher salt
¼	teaspoon coarsely ground black pepper
2	tablespoons flour
1½	cups chicken broth
1	can (about 15 ounces) diced tomatoes, preferably fire roasted, with their juice
1	can (about 15 ounces) white beans, such as Great Northern, drained and rinsed
1	ounce bittersweet chocolate, broken into pieces
2	tablespoons chopped fresh cilantro

HEAT the oil in a large deep skillet over medium-high heat. Add the chicken and sauté until it loses its raw look, about 3 minutes. Transfer to a 5- to 6-quart slow cooker.

ADD the onion to the oil remaining in the skillet and sauté until tender, about 2 minutes. Add the garlic, cumin, oregano, thyme, chili powder, cinnamon, salt, pepper, and flour and stir until the onion is evenly coated. Cook for 1 minute,

stirring constantly. Add the broth and tomatoes and stir until the liquid boils and thickens; transfer to the slow cooker. Add the beans, cover the cooker, and cook for 3 to 4 hours on high, or 6 to 8 hours on low.

REDUCE the cooker to warm. Add the chocolate and cilantro and stir until the chocolate melts, about 2 minutes. Serve immediately or hold on warm for up to 2 hours.

what else?

- Although this recipe is more silky than spicy, feel free to cut the amount of chili powder if your guests like flavors on the mild side. If you want to raise the heat, make your adjustments after the chili is cooked. Fiery flavors tend to explode during slow cooking.

- The amount of chocolate in the recipe is subtle, but its effect can be altered by using a sweeter chocolate for the kids, or a darker chocolate when serving adults only.

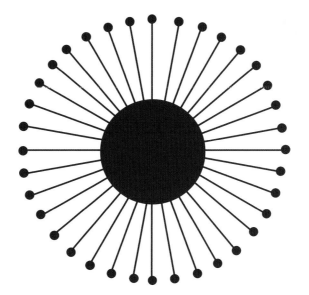

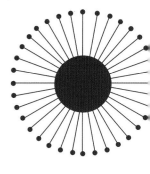

Bean Soup Ad Infinitum

This simple soup is designed to be versatile. Made exclusively from ingredients found in a well-stocked pantry, the basic version contains nothing perishable. It is perfect for a spur-of-the-moment dinner or an all-day cooking project, when inclement weather makes house arrest the ultimate luxury. Although delicious on its own, the real attraction of this shape-shifting recipe is its predisposition to endless variation. Feel free to embellish its prosaic purity with fresh vegetables, smoked meats, shredded cheese, or all of these. (See the Ad Infinitum Table on page 28 for more ideas.)

12

SERVINGS

PRECOOK

5 minutes

SLOW COOK

2 to 3 hours on high, or 4 to 8 hours on low, in a 5- to 6-quart slow cooker

AT THE END

20 minutes

1	tablespoon vegetable oil
1	medium onion, chopped
½	teaspoon dried thyme
1	can (about 15 ounces) white beans, drained and rinsed
1	can (about 15 ounces) chickpeas, drained and rinsed
1	can (about 15 ounces) red kidney beans, drained and rinsed

1	can (about 15 ounces) crushed tomatoes
4	cups chicken, vegetable, or beef broth
2	cups 100% vegetable juice, such as V8
2	bay leaves
1	teaspoon kosher salt
½	teaspoon coarsely ground black pepper
1	can (about 15 ounces) refried beans
2	tablespoons chopped fresh cilantro or Italian (flat-leaf) parsley (optional)

HEAT the oil in a medium skillet over medium heat. Add the onion and thyme and sauté until barely tender, about 3 minutes.

TRANSFER to a 5- to 6-quart slow cooker and add the white beans, chickpeas, kidney beans, tomatoes, broth, vegetable juice, bay leaves, salt, and pepper. Stir to combine, cover the cooker, and cook for 2 to 3 hours on high, or 4 to 8 hours on low, until the flavors are well blended.

IF THE COOKER IS ON LOW, raise the temperature to high. Mix the refried beans and a few ladlefuls of soup in a small bowl until the mixture is the consistency of thick cream. Return to the cooker and cook on high for 20 minutes, or until the soup is slightly thickened. Stir in the cilantro or parsley, if using. Remove the bay leaves before serving.

what else?

- Alter the types of beans you use to fit whatever you have on hand; any combination of canned beans will work well and cook in the same amount of time.

- If you don't have V8, add 1 cup each finely chopped carrot and celery to the onion, sauté, and add ½ cup tomato juice or an additional ½ cup canned crushed tomatoes with the beans.

- If you don't have refried beans, you can substitute a can of beans that have been drained, rinsed, and mashed, or stir ⅓ cup instant refried beans, black beans, hummus, or falafel mix into the soup 5 minutes before the end of cooking.

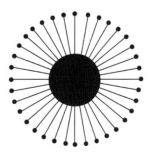

ad infinitum table

ADD		WHEN
1	carrot and 1 celery rib, ¼-inch dice	with onion
2	cups diced smoked ham	with the beans
4	strips bacon, finely chopped, cooked crisp with rendered fat	replace oil
2	ribs fennel, diced	with onion
4	garlic cloves, finely chopped	with onion
1	can (11 ounces) corn kernels, drained	with refried beans
1	large apple, peeled, cored, cut into ½-inch dice, sautéed in butter	with refried beans
1½	cups shredded cheddar	at serving
1	chipotle chile in adobo, finely chopped	with refried beans
1	tablespoon curry powder	with bay leaves

Manhattan Clam Chowder

Seafood soups don't need a slow cooker. Fish falls apart and shellfish gets rubbery when cooked all day, and seafood broth really doesn't need hours of cooking to reach perfection. And yet, the notion of 20 minutes of prep in the morning yielding an impressive, home-cooked indulgence at the end of the day, when it's most appreciated, is practically irresistible. In this recipe, fresh clams are steamed open in a mixture of wine and water and then reserved. The clam cooking liquid becomes the broth for the soup, eliminating the need for expensive and overly salty bottled clam juice. Because the clams are precooked, they only need to be warmed in the broth just before serving.

1	cup dry white wine
2	cups water
3	dozen littleneck clams, cleaned (clams should be tightly closed)
3	strips bacon, cut into ¼-inch dice
2	medium onions, cut into ¼-inch dice
2	celery ribs, cut into ¼-inch slices
½	green bell pepper, cut into ¼-inch dice
½	teaspoon dried oregano
½	teaspoon dried basil
1	teaspoon kosher salt
¼	teaspoon ground black pepper
1	bay leaf
1	can (about 28 ounces) diced tomatoes, drained
1	cup vegetable juice, such as V8
2	small red-skin or golden potatoes, peeled and cut into ¼-inch dice
2	tablespoons chopped fresh Italian (flat-leaf) parsley

6

SERVINGS

PRECOOK
15 minutes

SLOW COOK
4 to 6 hours on high, or 8 to 10 hours on low, in a 5- to 6-quart slow cooker

BRING the wine and water to a boil over high heat in a large deep skillet with a tight-fitting lid. Add the clams, cover, and boil until the clams open, 4 to 8 minutes. With a slotted spoon, remove the clams to a bowl as soon as they open and set aside. (Discard any unopened clams.) Strain the cooking liquid through a damp coffee filter or several layers of damp cheesecloth to remove grit, and reserve. You should have about 3 cups; add water if you have less.

WIPE out the skillet and cook the bacon over medium heat until crisp. Add the onions, celery, and bell pepper and cook until tender, about 3 minutes. Add the oregano, basil, salt, and pepper and sauté for 1 minute, stirring often. Transfer to a 5- to 6-quart slow cooker. Add the bay leaf, tomatoes, vegetable juice, potatoes, and the reserved clam cooking liquid, cover the cooker, and cook for 4 to 6 hours on high, or 8 to 10 hours on low.

WHILE THE SOUP IS COOKING, remove the clams from their shells; chop coarsely if large. Mix with any juice that drips from the shells. Refrigerate until the soup is done cooking.

WHEN THE SOUP IS DONE, remove the bay leaf and stir in the parsley and the clams with their juice.

CONTINUED

Manhattan Clam Chowder <small>CONTINUED</small>

what else?

- You can use canned clams, if you can't find fresh, but then replace the clam cooking liquid with bottled clam juice.

- If you can't find littleneck clams, any variety will do. Large clams, like cherrystones or sea clams, will need a longer initial cooking time to open.

- This soup is equally good made with mussels instead of clams. If using mussels, double the amount and precook them for about half the time.

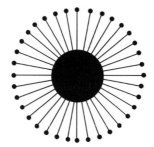

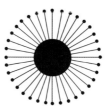

Creamy Onion Soup

If your idea of onion soup is the crocked restaurant variety, brothy, beefy, and capped with Gruyère, then I'd like to introduce you to its thick and creamy cousin. Enriched with cream cheese and pudgy from shredded potato, the soup naturally thickens as it simmers. It makes a spectacular lunch or a first course for a light dinner, and converts effortlessly into a main course with the addition of diced ham, smoked salmon, or grilled chicken.

8

SERVINGS

PRECOOK

15 minutes

SLOW COOK

3 to 4 hours on high, or 6 to 8 hours on low, in a 5- to 6-quart slow cooker

AT THE END

15 minutes

2	tablespoons vegetable oil
2	pounds onions (about 4 large onions), cut into ½-inch dice
¾	cups dry white wine
5	cups vegetable or chicken broth
1	pound boiling potatoes (such as golden), peeled and coarsely shredded
1	teaspoon kosher salt
¼	teaspoon coarsely ground black pepper
½	teaspoon dried dill weed
¼	teaspoon dried thyme
4	ounces cream cheese, softened
1	cup low-fat milk, divided

HEAT the oil in a large skillet over medium heat. Add the onions and sauté until very lightly browned, about 5 minutes, stirring often. Add the wine and boil until reduced by half, about 3 minutes.

MEANWHILE, bring the broth to a boil in a saucepan; stir in the potatoes and return to a boil. Transfer the broth and potato mixture and the cooked onion to a 5- to 6-quart slow cooker. Stir in the salt, pepper, dill, and thyme. Cover the cooker and cook for 3 to 4 hours on high, or 6 to 8 hours on low, until the potatoes and onions are very tender.

WHISK together the cream cheese and ¼ cup of the milk in a small bowl until thoroughly combined. Whisk in the remaining ¾ cup milk until smooth. Stir into the soup and heat through on low for about 15 minutes.

what else?

- To make a smoked salmon and dill soup, add 4 to 6 ounces finely chopped smoked salmon along with the milk; double the amount of dill.

- For a milder flavor, substitute chopped white parts of leeks for half the onion.

- For a pungent, cheesy soup, replace the cream cheese with crumbled blue cheese or shredded smoked cheddar.

- For a smoky flavor, replace the oil with 2 slices finely chopped bacon, and cook the bacon until crisp before adding the onion.

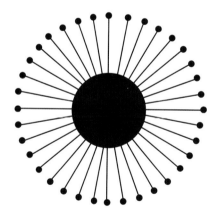

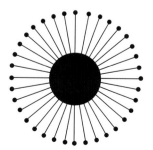

Corn Chowder with Jalapeño

Jalapeños used to be the "poster peppers" for heat; not so anymore. Tamed and mass-produced, the flame of jalapeños has been tempered to titillate rather than burn. Normally I refrain from adding chiles to slow cooker recipes until the very end, to keep their heat from taking over, but in this recipe I add them at the start. This is partly to allow the reengineered, tamer jalapeños time to gain some punch, but it is also to ensure that the flavor of chile radiates through the soup. Every bite should provide a tingle; every bowl should leave your lips with a characteristic jalapeño glow. The recipe calls for either 2 or 3 jalapeños, depending on how hot you like your chowder.

8

SERVINGS

PRECOOK

15 minutes

SLOW COOK

3 to 4 hours on high, or 6 to 8 hours on low, in a 5- to 6-quart slow cooker

AT THE END

1 minute

2	slices salt pork or bacon, finely diced
2	onions, finely chopped
1	bell pepper, red or green, stemmed, seeded, and finely diced
2	celery ribs, finely diced
2 to 3	jalapeño peppers, stemmed, seeded, and finely chopped
3	cups corn kernels (about two 11-ounce cans), drained
1	can (about 15 ounces) diced tomatoes, preferably fire roasted
1	can (about 15 ounces) cannellini beans, drained and rinsed
2	tablespoons yellow cornmeal
1	teaspoon kosher salt
½	teaspoon coarsely cracked black pepper
1	teaspoon ground cumin, preferably ground from whole seeds toasted in a dry skillet
1	teaspoon dried oregano
1	teaspoon chopped fresh rosemary
5	cups vegetable or chicken broth
1	cup cream or half-and-half

HEAT a large deep skillet, preferably cast-iron, over medium-high heat. Add the salt pork and cook until browned and the bottom of the pan is glazed with fat. Add the onions, bell pepper, celery, and jalapeños, and sauté until the onions are lightly browned and tender, about 5 minutes. Transfer to a 5- to 6-quart slow cooker, and add the corn, tomatoes, and beans.

ADD the cornmeal, salt, pepper, cumin, oregano, and rosemary to the skillet and cook for 30 seconds over medium heat, stirring constantly. Add the broth and heat to boiling, stirring often. Continue boiling until thickened, stirring constantly, for about 2 minutes, and pour into the slow cooker. Cover the cooker and cook for 3 to 4 hours on high, or 6 to 8 hours on low, until the vegetables are tender and the flavors are blended.

STIR in the cream and heat through, about 1 minute.

what else?

- The cornmeal thickens the soup and adds an appealing grainy texture. If you don't have cornmeal, substitute 1 tablespoon flour; it will thicken just as well. Or you can throw in a handful of crumbled corn chips once you add the broth. If you do use the corn chips, don't wait for the broth to thicken in the skillet. Just add everything to the slow cooker and the chips will thicken the soup as it cooks.

- If you love chiles, feel free to add something spicier, like a minced habanero or Scotch Bonnet, about 10 minutes before the soup is done cooking.

Herby Minestrone

Vegetable soups provide the most flexible timing of any slow-cooker recipe. Vegetable fiber holds up well to low moist heat, yielding the aromas and nutrients of the vegetables into the broth gradually. This herbaceous soup is loaded with vegetables and flavor. It can be ready in as little as 3 hours or as long as 10, which makes it perfect for any schedule your time-crunched life demands.

2	tablespoons extra-virgin olive oil		½	teaspoon dried sage
1	large onion, cut into ½-inch dice		4	cups beef or vegetable broth
3	carrots, peeled and cut into ½-inch-thick slices		1	can (about 15 ounces) chickpeas, drained and rinsed
2	celery ribs, cut into ½-inch-thick slices		1	cup 100% vegetable juice, such as V8
2	yellow bell peppers, stemmed, seeded, and halved		1	can (about 28 ounces) diced tomatoes
3	cloves garlic, minced, divided		1	tablespoon red wine vinegar
1	teaspoon chopped fresh savory		½	teaspoon kosher salt
1	teaspoon chopped fresh rosemary		¼	teaspoon ground black pepper
1	teaspoon chopped fresh thyme		¼	cup chopped fresh Italian (flat-leaf) parsley
½	teaspoon dried oregano			Juice and finely grated zest of ½ lemon
½	teaspoon dried basil		½	cup shredded Parmigiano-Reggiano cheese

HEAT the oil in a large skillet over medium-high heat. Add the onion, carrots, celery, and bell peppers and sauté until the vegetables lose their raw look, about 3 minutes. Add 2 cloves of the garlic, the savory, rosemary, thyme, oregano, basil, and sage and cook for another minute. Transfer to a 5- to 6-quart slow cooker.

ADD the broth, chickpeas, vegetable juice, diced tomatoes, vinegar, salt, and pepper. Cover the cooker and cook for 3 to 5 hours on high, or 6 to 10 hours on low.

STIR in the parsley, the remaining garlic clove, and the lemon juice and lemon zest. Serve, garnished with shredded cheese.

8-10
SERVINGS

PRECOOK
5 minutes

SLOW COOK
3 to 5 hours on high, or 6 to 10 hours on low, in a 5- to 6-quart slow cooker

AT THE END
1 minute

what else?

- Minestrone improves with age; for the best flavor, prepare a day or two ahead. Or cook overnight, refrigerate until dinner, and reheat on the stove top.

- Feel free to alter the mix of vegetables you use to fit whatever you have on hand.

Moroccan Red Lentil Soup

Forget your "same old, same old" lentil soup and take a deep breath. Can you smell the cumin, the coriander, the whiff of cinnamon? Open your eyes and take in the burnt-orange glow of turmeric burnished with tomatoes and sweet paprika. Lentil soups may come and go, but this exotic concoction will stick in your memory, not just for its heady aromas and hearty texture, but also for its ease and versatility. Unlike dried beans, red lentils don't need to be soaked before they're cooked.

6
SERVINGS

PRECOOK
10 minutes

SLOW COOK
4 to 5 hours on high, or 8 to 10 hours on low, in a 5- to 6-quart slow cooker

AT THE END
10 minutes

2	tablespoons extra-virgin olive oil
2	large onions, cut into medium dice
2	cloves garlic, minced
2	teaspoons ground coriander
1	teaspoon ground cumin, preferably ground from whole seeds toasted in a dry skillet
1	teaspoon ground turmeric
½	teaspoon paprika
¼	teaspoon ground cinnamon
1½	teaspoons kosher salt
½	teaspoon ground black pepper
7	cups vegetable broth
1	can (about 20 ounces) crushed tomatoes
2	cups dried red lentils, washed and rinsed
	Pinch of red pepper flakes
	Juice of 1 lemon
3	tablespoons fresh Italian (flat-leaf) parsley
1	tablespoon chopped fresh cilantro

HEAT the olive oil in a large skillet over medium-high heat. Add the onions and cook until tender, about 3 minutes. Add the garlic, coriander, cumin, turmeric, paprika, cinnamon, salt, and pepper and cook for another minute. Add the broth and tomatoes and heat to boiling. Pour into a 5- to 6-quart slow cooker. Stir in the lentils, cover the cooker, and cook for 4 to 5 hours on high, or 8 to 10 hours on low, until the lentils are tender.

STIR in the pepper flakes, lemon juice, parsley, and cilantro, cover, and cook on high for 10 minutes.

what else?

- Before sautéing the onion, sauté 1 pound boneless, skinless dark chicken meat or leg of lamb, cut into ½-inch pieces, in the oil until browned. Add the onion to the pan and proceed with the recipe.

- Substitute 2 cups small dried white beans, soaked overnight, for the lentils.

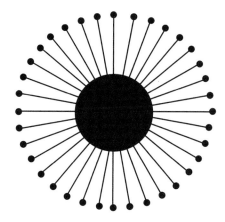

Wild Mushroom and Wild Rice Bisque

Extreme elegance meets stick-to-the-ribs heartiness in this robust soup. It calls for a combination of dried wild mushrooms and fresh exotic ones. Most of the fresh mushrooms sold as "wild" in your supermarket are actually cultivated mushrooms, similar to the common white button mushroom, but because they have more flavor, a meatier texture, and are generally darker in color, we use them like the foraged wild mushrooms they resemble. Wild rice is a prime candidate for slow cooking. Its tough hull helps it remain appealingly chewy, even after hours of cooking.

1	tablespoon extra-virgin olive oil
1	large onion, cut into ½-inch dice
1	large carrot, peeled and cut into ¼-inch-thick slices
1	large celery rib, cut into ¼-inch-thick slices
1	pound cremini (baby portobello) mushrooms, cut into slices
1	clove garlic, finely chopped
½	teaspoon dried thyme
½	teaspoon dried rosemary, crushed
½	cup wild rice, rinsed
½	ounce dried wild mushrooms, any type, minced
6	cups beef broth
1	cup canned diced tomatoes
1	teaspoon kosher salt
¼	teaspoon coarsely ground black pepper
3	tablespoons instant mashed potato flakes
1	tablespoon chopped fresh Italian (flat-leaf) parsley

HEAT the oil in a large skillet over medium-high heat. Add the onion, carrot, celery, and cremini mushrooms and sauté until the vegetables brown lightly, about 6 minutes. Add the garlic, thyme, and rosemary and cook for another minute. Transfer to a 5- to 6-quart slow cooker.

ADD the wild rice, dried wild mushrooms, beef broth, tomatoes, salt, and pepper. Cover the cooker and cook on high for 4 hours, or on low for 6 to 8 hours, until the wild rice is tender.

STIR in the potato flakes and parsley and cook on high for 10 minutes.

6
SERVINGS

PRECOOK
10 minutes

SLOW COOK
4 hours on high, or 6 to 8 hours on low, in a 5- to 6-quart slow cooker

AT THE END
10 minutes

what else?

- Like most soups, this one improves with age; for the best flavor, prepare a day or two ahead, or cook overnight and refrigerate until dinner. As the soup sits, the rice will absorb more of the broth, so you may need to add a bit more broth when you reheat the soup.

- To make the soup vegetarian, substitute mushroom or vegetable broth for the beef broth.

Curried Coconut Chicken Soup

As a rule, boneless, skinless chicken breast does not do well in a slow cooker. Its lean, pale fibers are designed for a speedy sauté or a quick turn under a broiler, rather than a prolonged simmer. And yet it is so ubiquitous in the modern kitchen that I felt compelled to find a way to use it to its best advantage in this book. This soup is the result. I tried it first with boneless thighs, which are usually preferable when slow-cooking, but found they made a gamey broth. The chicken breast did just the opposite; the broth was clean and sweet, the perfect background for an exotic flavoring of ginger, curry, coconut milk, and lemongrass.

6

SERVINGS

PRECOOK

15 minutes

SLOW COOK

3 to 5 hours on high, or 4 to 8 hours on low, in a 5- to 6-quart slow cooker

AT THE END

15 minutes

2	tablespoons vegetable oil, divided
1½	pounds boneless, skinless chicken breast, cut into ½-inch cubes
2	medium onions, cut into ¼-inch dice
1	carrot, peeled and cut into thin slices
½	red bell pepper, cut into ¼-by-1-inch strips
4	cloves garlic, minced
1	tablespoon minced gingerroot
1	tablespoon Madras curry powder
4	cups chicken broth
1	teaspoon kosher salt
3	large stalks lemongrass, trimmed and cut into thin slices (see Trimming Lemongrass, page 44)
1	can (about 14 ounces) coconut milk
2	tablespoons creamy peanut butter
2	teaspoons soy sauce
2	teaspoons hot pepper sauce, such as Sriracha
1	teaspoon light brown sugar
¼	cup coarsely chopped fresh cilantro leaves

HEAT half the oil in a large deep skillet over medium heat. Sauté the chicken in 2 batches until it is lightly browned, about 4 minutes per batch; transfer to a 5- to 6-quart slow cooker.

ADD the remaining oil to the skillet and heat. Add the onions, carrot, and bell pepper and sauté until almost tender, about 3 minutes. Stir in the garlic, ginger, and curry powder and cook for a few seconds, until aromatic. Add the broth, salt, and lemongrass and heat to boiling. Pour into the slow cooker, cover, and cook for 3 to 5 hours on high, or 4 to 8 hours on low, until the broth is full-flavored and the vegetables are all tender.

MEANWHILE, mix the coconut milk, peanut butter, soy sauce, hot pepper sauce, and brown sugar to combine. Pour into the cooked soup and cook on high for 15 minutes. Stir in the cilantro and serve.

2/24/13 - soooooo good - def make again. Could leave out 2c. of broth & serve over rice as a curry w/thick sauce.

what else?

- Turkey breast may be substituted for chicken breast.

- Feel free to use leftover cooked chicken breast in place of the fresh chicken. If you do, skip the first cooking step.

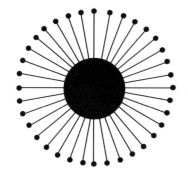
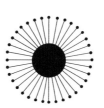
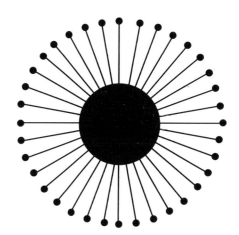

trimming lemongrass

The outside of lemongrass is tough—so tough that no amount of boiling will tenderize its fibers. In order to use it in a soup, you must either steep it in broth, discarding it once its flavor is extracted, or trim it severely down to its tender white core. To trim lemongrass, cut off the stubby root end and peel away the strawlike leaves wrapped tightly around the core. You know you have gone far enough when you have removed a purple-tinged layer surrounding the creamy white core. Slice the core into paper-thin slices.

Winter Fruit Soup

Forget your chicken soup and the megadoses of vitamin C and zinc. This pungent, fragrant soup is all you need to cure anything from the common cold to mild depression. Faintly intoxicating, radiating cinnamon, lemon, and thyme, and plush with fruit, this elixir is pure comfort food. Serve it warm before a winter stew or roast, or chilled as a dessert dolloped with a scoop of ice cream.

1	bottle fruity red wine, such as Merlot or Shiraz
½	cup sugar
	Pinch of salt
3	tablespoons instant tapioca, or 2 tablespoons tapioca starch
3	cups water, divided
24	dried whole apricots, quartered

16	pitted prunes, quartered
2	cinnamon sticks
1	cup unsweetened applesauce
¾	cup golden raisins, dried cranberries, and/or currants, in any combination
	Juice and finely grated zest of ½ lemon
	Leaves from 2 small sprigs fresh thyme

BRING the wine to a boil in a large saucepan over medium-high heat and boil for 3 minutes. Add the sugar and salt, and stir until the sugar dissolves.

SOFTEN the tapioca in ½ cup of the water for about 5 minutes. Stir into the wine and heat until the mixture thickens slightly, stirring often. Combine the wine mixture, apricots, prunes, cinnamon, applesauce, the raisins, cranberries, and/or currants, and the remaining 2½ cups water in a 5- to 6-quart slow cooker. Cover the cooker and cook for 3 to 4 hours on high, or 6 to 8 hours on low.

REMOVE the cinnamon sticks and discard. Stir in the lemon juice and zest and the thyme and cook for at least 5 more minutes before serving.

8

SERVINGS

PRECOOK
15 minutes

SLOW COOK
3 to 4 hours on high, or 6 to 8 hours on low, in a 5- to 6-quart slow cooker

AT THE END
5 minutes

Parmigiano Pumpkin Soup
with Frizzled Prosciutto

If your notion of pumpkin is "sweet," and if you think it should be seasoned only with nutmeg, clove, cinnamon, and sugar, then get ready to change your mind. This savory, creamy, pungently cheesy pumpkin soup is fragrant with garlic and Parmesan, and punctuated with the frizzled threads of crisped prosciutto. Serve it as a first course before a roast (it makes an inspired appetizer for Thanksgiving), or for lunch with someone you're dying to impress.

2	tablespoons extra-virgin olive oil
2	ounces thinly sliced prosciutto, cut into thin strips
1	large onion, cut into ⅛-inch dice
3	cloves garlic, minced
1	can (about 28 ounces) 100% pure pumpkin
2	quarts vegetable or chicken broth
⅛	teaspoon ground nutmeg
1	teaspoon kosher salt
½	teaspoon ground white pepper
½	cup cream (at least 10% fat)
½	cup freshly grated Parmigiano-Reggiano cheese
2	tablespoons chopped fresh Italian (flat-leaf) parsley

SERVINGS

PRECOOK
10 minutes

SLOW COOK
3 to 4 hours on high, or 6 to 8 hours on low, in a 5- to 6-quart slow cooker

AT THE END
5 minutes

HEAT the oil in a large deep skillet over medium-high heat. Add the prosciutto and sauté until crisp and frizzled, about 1 minute. Remove with a slotted spoon and reserve.

REDUCE the heat to medium, add the onion to the skillet, and sauté until tender (do not brown), about 3 minutes. Add the garlic and cook for a few seconds, until aromatic. Stir in the pumpkin, broth, nutmeg, salt, and pepper and bring to a boil. Transfer to a 5- to 6-quart slow cooker, cover, and cook for 3 to 4 hours on high, or 6 to 8 hours on low.

STIR in the cream and Parmesan and heat through, about 5 minutes. Stir in the parsley and garnish with the frizzled prosciutto.

CONTINUED

Parmigiano Pumpkin Soup
with Frizzled Prosciutto CONTINUED

> ## what else?
>
> - Even though the length of cooking time for this soup would make it possible to use fresh pumpkin instead of canned, I advise you not to. Libby's canned pumpkin (the most commonly available brand) is made from a specially cultivated strain of pumpkin designed for cooking. It is richer, creamier, and tastier than any fresh pumpkin you can purchase.
>
> - If you don't have prosciutto, you can substitute 3 slices bacon, cut into thin strips.
>
> - Feel free to alter the type of cheese you use to fit your taste or whatever you have on hand. Any smoked cheese would be delicious in the soup, and other grating cheeses, like Asiago or Romano, are easy to find.

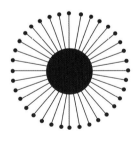

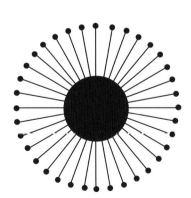

Roasted Vegetable Soup

Roasting vegetables does more than simply cook them. It transforms them into something savory and sweet, meaty and voluptuous—not the sort of attributes one usually ascribes to produce. This otherwise straightforward vegetarian vegetable soup benefits from the transformation. Although it takes 30 minutes of roasting before you start slow-cooking, the process is largely untended, and the roasting can be done days ahead.

2   onions, cut into 1-inch dice

2   carrots, peeled and cut into 1-inch sticks

2   celery ribs, cut into ½-inch-thick slices

1   medium turnip, peeled and cut into 1-inch dice

½   red bell pepper, cut into 1-inch squares

1   small sweet potato, peeled and cut into 1-inch dice

8   white mushrooms, cleaned and quartered

4   large cloves garlic, whole and unpeeled

2   tablespoons extra-virgin olive oil

6   cups vegetable broth, divided

1   can (about 15 ounces) diced tomatoes, preferably fire roasted, with their juice

1   teaspoon kosher salt

½   teaspoon ground black pepper

½   teaspoon dried rosemary, crushed

½   teaspoon dried thyme

2   tablespoons chopped fresh Italian (flat-leaf) parsley

3   tablespoons couscous, preferably whole-wheat

6

SERVINGS

PRECOOK

30 minutes

SLOW COOK

2 to 3 hours on high, or 4 to 6 hours on low, in a 5- to 6-quart slow cooker

AT THE END

5 minutes

PREHEAT an oven to 425°F. Toss the onions, carrots, celery, turnip, bell pepper, sweet potato, mushrooms, and garlic with the olive oil on a large rimmed sheet pan. Spread out into an even layer and roast for 30 minutes, or until the vegetables are tender and lightly browned at the edges.

SCRAPE the vegetables into a 5- to 6-quart slow cooker. Pour 1 cup of the vegetable broth onto the sheet pan and scrape up any browned bits clinging to it; scrape into the cooker. Add the remaining 5 cups broth, the diced tomatoes and their juice, the salt, pepper, rosemary, and thyme. Cover the cooker and cook for 2 to 3 hours on high, or 4 to 6 hours on low, until the flavors are blended.

STIR in the parsley and couscous and cook for 5 more minutes.

CONTINUED

Roasted Vegetable Soup CONTINUED

what else?

- Feel free to alter the selection of vegetables you use to fit your taste and whatever you have on hand, but try to keep the volume of vegetables approximately the same.

- Like most soups, this one benefits from age. The flavor will improve after it sits for a day.

- Garnish with grated cheese, if desired.

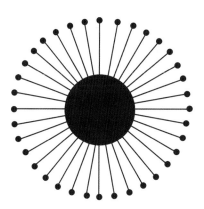

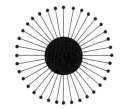

The Bottomless Stew Pot

STEW TAKES ITS TIME: time to trim and cut the ingredients, time to brown the meat properly, but mostly time to stew. It won't be rushed or accommodate shortcuts, and it doesn't care how pressed or harried the cook is. A stew relaxes until it's done, and we have no choice but to do the same.

The slow cooker is a natural for stew, for it is through long, gentle cooking that stew meat melts into luscious morsels and the flavor of the broth takes on body and depth. But before simmering comes an equally important step—browning.

Stew meats pose a unique challenge to the browning process. Because the meat is in pieces, there are many surfaces that need browning and through which liquid is apt to seep. The main tricks are to keep the pan hot and to avoid crowding it.

When meat browns, it always secretes some moisture, even if it has been floured. If the amount isn't large, the droplets of meat juices falling into the hot pan vaporize and dissipate into the air. However, if the skillet is crowded and the chunks of meat touch, the moisture they emit gets trapped between the pieces, where it steams, thus preventing the meat from browning. So, unless you have a super-sized skillet, you should plan to brown meat in batches; it won't take much longer, and you'll get far better results.

Stew is finished when its ingredients are fork-tender. If you're around, you can test it with a prod after about four hours and every hour after that until it's ready. Or the stew can simmer unobserved until you're ready to eat. I suppose it's possible to over-cook a stew, but it would take such disregard that the mishap would border on culinary neglect.

CHAPTER 2

Recipes

Chicken Cacciatore

In the ancient world, the best meat never made it home for cooking; it was eaten on the spot by hunters in the field. *Cacciatore*, which means "hunter" in Italian, is such a preparation. Traditionally a stew of game, forest herbs, foraged mushrooms, wild onions, and a shot of whatever alcoholic sustenance the hunter had on hand, cacciatore was primal nourishment. It still is, and it's a perfect choice for slow-cooking. The only hitch is that cacciatore has migrated over the centuries from game meat to chicken, an animal that lends itself only partially to stewing. The dark meat (especially the thighs) stews beautifully; the white meat withers. Choose chicken thighs still on the bone for maximum flavor and succulence, but remove the skin, because it will become flabby during cooking. Cacciatore yields an abundance of delicious gravy, so serve it with noodles, rice, or lots of bread to soak up all of the goodness.

SERVINGS

PRECOOK

20 minutes

SLOW COOK

3 to 4 hours on high, or 5 to 8 hours on low, in a 5- to 6-quart slow cooker

AT THE END

5 minutes

⅓	cup flour
1	teaspoon kosher salt
½	teaspoon coarsely ground black pepper
2	teaspoons poultry seasoning
4	pounds skinless chicken thighs (about 8), bone-in
2 to 3	tablespoons extra-virgin olive oil, divided
1	onion, coarsely chopped
1	pound mushrooms, cut into thick slices

2	cloves garlic, minced
¼	teaspoon dried oregano
1	teaspoon chopped fresh rosemary, or dried rosemary, crushed
1	cup chicken broth
1	cup canned diced tomatoes, drained
1	tablespoon minced anchovy fillet or anchovy paste
2	tablespoon chopped fresh Italian (flat-leaf) parsley

MIX the flour, salt, pepper, and poultry seasoning in a medium mixing bowl. Turn the chicken thighs in the flour mixture until thoroughly coated; pat off the excess flour and reserve the seasoned flour mixture.

HEAT 1 tablespoon oil in a large deep skillet over medium-high heat. Brown the chicken in batches, about 3 minutes per side. Do not crowd the pan, and add more oil if the pan becomes dry.

Transfer the browned chicken to a 5- to 6-quart slow cooker as it is browned.

ADD more oil to the skillet, if needed, and heat over medium heat. Add the onion and mushrooms and sauté until the vegetables are tender, stirring often, about 4 minutes. Add the garlic, oregano, and rosemary and sauté for another minute.

ADD the reserved seasoned flour and stir until the vegetables are coated. Add the chicken broth and tomatoes and heat until thickened, stirring often and scraping up any browned bits clinging to the bottom of the pan. Pour into the slow cooker, cover the cooker, and cook for 3 to 4 hours on high, or 5 to 8 hours on low, until the chicken is easily pierced with a fork.

REMOVE the chicken to a platter with a slotted spoon. Stir the anchovies and parsley into the sauce and simmer for 5 minutes. Spoon the sauce over the chicken and serve with hot cooked pasta, rice, or bread.

what else?

- You may substitute turkey thighs or cut-up rabbit for the chicken thighs.

- Serve the cacciatore with Mushroom-Barley Risotto (page 168) on special occasions.

- Like all stews, cacciatore gets better with age. Refrigerate for up to 2 days and reheat in a large saucepan or in a 350°F oven in a covered baking dish.

Turkey and Cranberry Pot Pie

Pot pies are nothing more than stews topped with pastry. They tend toward the labor-intensive end of the convenience cooking spectrum, but the slow cooker (and the life-saving assistance of refrigerated piecrust) streamlines the problem areas dramatically. The real secret is in the thermodynamic properties of the slow-cooker crock. The crock of a slow cooker is designed to heat gradually and hold onto its heat for a long time. Because of that, you can top any stew made in a slow cooker with pastry, biscuit dough, or dumplings right in the crock, and pop it in a hot oven to brown. The presentation is impressive, and the technique couldn't be easier.

SERVINGS

PRECOOK
20 minutes

SLOW COOK
3 to 4 hours on high,
or 6 to 8 hours on
low, in a 5- to 6-quart
slow cooker

AT THE END
25 minutes

⅓	cup flour
1	teaspoon kosher salt
¼	teaspoon coarsely ground black pepper
2	teaspoons poultry seasoning
2½	pounds boneless, skinless turkey thighs, cut into 1-inch pieces
2 to 3	tablespoons vegetable oil, divided
2	onions, chopped
2	carrots, peeled and cut into thin slices
2	celery ribs, cut into thin slices
8	medium mushrooms, cut into slices
2	red-skin or golden potatoes, peeled and cut into ½-inch dice
1½	cups chicken broth
⅓	cup dried cranberries
	Pie dough for a 9-inch piecrust, prepared refrigerated or homemade

MIX the flour, salt, pepper, and poultry seasoning in a medium-large mixing bowl. Add the turkey meat and toss until the pieces are thoroughly coated; pat off the excess flour and reserve the seasoned flour mixture.

HEAT 1 tablespoon oil in a large deep skillet over medium-high heat. Brown the turkey pieces in batches, about 2 minutes per side; do not crowd the pan, and add more oil if the pan becomes dry. Transfer the browned turkey to a 5- to 6-quart slow cooker as it is browned.

ADD more oil to the skillet, if needed, and heat over medium heat. Add the onions, carrots, celery, mushrooms, and potatoes and sauté until the vegetables lose their raw look, stirring often, about 4 minutes.

ADD the reserved seasoned flour mixture and stir until the vegetables are well coated. Add the chicken broth and heat to boiling, stirring constantly, until the sauce is slightly thickened. Transfer to the slow cooker, add the dried cranberries, and stir to mix well. Cover the cooker and cook for 3 to 4 hours on high, or 6 to 8 hours on low.

CONTINUED

Turkey and Cranberry Pot Pie CONTINUED

PREHEAT an oven to 375°F. Roll the dough out on a lightly floured work surface. Remove the lid from the cooker and dry it with a paper towel. Lay the lid on the dough and use it as a template to cut the dough in the shape of the lid. Roll up the edges of the dough all the way around so that the dough will fit neatly over the turkey stew. Remove the crock from the slow cooker and lay the dough on top of the stew. Cut several slits in the middle of the crust and bake until browned, about 25 minutes. Serve immediately.

what else?

- Make a homier version of pot pie using biscuit dough rather than pastry. Just make a batch of your favorite biscuit recipe (it's fine to use a mix). Roll out and cut to the shape of the crock or as individual biscuits and place on top. Bake as you would using the pie dough.

- You can also go opulent by replacing the piecrust with frozen puff pastry; bake according to the package directions.

New and Improved Irish Stew

Traditional Irish stew is pretty austere stuff—browned bits of lamb simmered with potatoes, onions, and carrots, with a smidgen of thyme for pizzazz. This one has a little more going on. The parsnips add sweetness, the turnip delivers some needed astringency, and a dash of Worcestershire tilts the whole thing dangerously close to delicious. It's enough to make your old Aunt Bridget a wee bit excited.

¼	cup flour
1	teaspoon kosher salt
¼	teaspoon coarsely ground black pepper
1	teaspoon dried thyme, divided
2	pounds boneless lamb cubes for stew
3	tablespoons vegetable oil, divided
2	medium onions, cut into 1-inch chunks
2	carrots, peeled and cut into ½-inch-thick slices

1	celery rib, cut into ½-inch-thick slices
1	turnip, peeled and cut into ¾-inch dice
2	parsnips, peeled and cut into ½-inch-thick slices
1	pound red-skin or golden potatoes, peeled and cut into ½-inch dice
1½	cups beef broth
1	tablespoon Worcestershire sauce or steak sauce, such as A-1

MIX the flour, salt, pepper, and ½ teaspoon thyme in a medium-large mixing bowl. Add the lamb and toss until the meat is evenly coated; pat off the excess flour and reserve the seasoned flour mixture.

HEAT half the oil in a large deep skillet over medium-high heat, and brown the lamb, about 3 minutes per side, in batches if necessary; do not crowd the pan. Transfer to a bowl, and set aside.

ADD the remaining oil to the skillet. Add the onions, carrots, celery, turnip, parsnips, and potatoes and sauté until browned and barely tender, about 6 minutes. Transfer to a 5- to 6-quart slow cooker; put the lamb on top.

ADD the reserved seasoned flour and remaining ½ teaspoon thyme to the skillet and cook over medium heat until the flour is lightly browned, about 1 minute. Add the broth, heat to a boil, and continue to cook, stirring constantly, until slightly thickened. Pour into the slow cooker. Cover and cook for 3 to 4 hours on high, or 6 to 8 hours on low, until the vegetables and lamb are tender.

ADD the Worcestershire or steak sauce, stir to blend, and serve.

SERVINGS

PRECOOK
20 minutes

SLOW COOK
3 to 4 hours on high, or 6 to 8 hours on low, in a 5- to 6-quart slow cooker

AT THE END
1 minute

Sweet Beef Goulash with Smoked Paprika

Smoked paprika, also known as *pimentón de la Vera,* is a signature Spanish spice. I realize it is probably heresy to employ its oaky, smoked nuance in the iconic stew of Hungary, the paprika capital of Europe, where the spice is taken very seriously and is never, ever smoked. So sue me; the results are unconventionally delicious. Smoked paprika comes in three varieties: sweet, semisweet, and hot. You want the sweet one here. Do not be alarmed by the lack of liquid in the recipe; the onions will melt into a thick, caramelized sauce that is impossible to achieve without spending hours of slow cooking. How convenient!

6 SERVINGS

PRECOOK
45 minutes

SLOW COOK
3 to 4 hours on high, or 6 to 8 hours on low, in a 5- to 6-quart slow cooker

AT THE END
5 minutes

6	large yellow (Spanish) onions, halved and cut into ¼-inch-thick slices	2½	pounds trimmed beef chuck, cut into chunks for stew
3	tablespoons vegetable oil, divided	1	tablespoon dark brown sugar
1	cup beef broth, divided	1	tablespoon ketchup
3	tablespoons flour	1	tablespoon cider vinegar
1	teaspoon caraway seed	1	tablespoon chopped fresh Italian (flat-leaf) parsley
3	tablespoons smoked paprika, divided		
1	teaspoon kosher salt		

PREHEAT an oven to 375°F. Toss the onions and 1 tablespoon oil on a large rimmed sheet pan. Roast until the onions are lightly browned, about 45 minutes, tossing once halfway through the roasting time. Remove from the oven and pour ½ cup beef broth over the onions, scraping up any browned bits clinging to the pan. Scrape into a 5- to 6-quart slow cooker.

WHILE THE ONIONS ROAST, mix the flour, caraway seed, 1 tablespoon paprika, and the salt in a medium mixing bowl. Add the beef and toss to coat evenly; pat off the excess flour and reserve the flour mixture.

HEAT 1 tablespoon oil in a large heavy skillet over medium-high heat and brown the beef on all sides in 2 batches, adding the remaining tablespoon of oil before the second batch. Transfer each batch of meat to the slow cooker after it browns.

ADD the reserved seasoned flour to the pan, and cook, stirring constantly, until lightly browned, about 4 minutes. Stir in the remaining ½ cup beef broth, the brown sugar, ketchup, vinegar, and 1 tablespoon of the remaining paprika. Bring to a boil, stirring constantly, then pour into the cooker. Cover the cooker and cook for 3 to 4 hours on high, or 6 to 8 hours on low, until the onions are practically liquefied and the beef is fork-tender.

STIR in the remaining tablespoon of paprika and the parsley and cook for 5 more minutes. Serve over wide egg noodles cooked according to the package directions, if desired.

what else?

- Although it may seem logical to use a "sweet" onion for a sweet goulash, resist the temptation. Onions bred to be sweet actually have less sugar by weight than standard yellow onions. They are only sweet to the extent that they lack pungency, which makes them great for eating raw, but dismal in a slow cooker, where they are simply bland.

- If you can't find smoked paprika, feel free to use sweet Hungarian paprika, which will also be delicious and much more authentic.

Sirloin Chili (No Beans)

In Texas, chili is served sidling up to the beans, never commingled. This chili is from that segregated tradition, and since it is all about the meat, I've replaced the ubiquitous ground beef of commonplace chilis with chunks of sirloin. Because the heat of chile peppers expands in the slow cooker, the aromatic parts of chili powder (cumin and oregano) are added at the beginning, but I've kept the ground chile peppers separate, adding them in the last 15 minutes. Any ground chile will work well in this recipe. Anchos are my old standby, but I've been known to replace them with other fairly mild chiles, like guajillo or New Mexico, or to turn up the heat by using a chipotle or habanero for part of the mix.

SERVINGS

PRECOOK

15 minutes

SLOW COOK

4 to 5 hours on high, or 8 to 9 hours on low, in a 3-quart, or larger, slow cooker

AT THE END

15 minutes

2	pounds sirloin steak, trimmed of fat and gristle and cut into 1-inch cubes
	Kosher salt
	Ground black pepper
2	tablespoons vegetable oil
1	large onion, diced
1	medium green bell pepper, stemmed, seeded, and cut into 1-inch pieces
2	fresh chile peppers (red or green), stemmed, seeded, and finely chopped
1	clove garlic, minced
1	tablespoon ground cumin, preferably ground from whole seeds toasted in a dry skillet
1	teaspoon dried oregano
2	tablespoons flour
1	cup beef broth
1½	cups crushed tomatoes, preferably fire-roasted
2	tablespoons ground chile (ancho, guajillo, and/or New Mexico)

SEASON the sirloin cubes with salt and pepper to taste. Heat the oil in a large skillet over medium-high heat and brown the beef in 2 batches, about 3 minutes per side, transferring each batch to a 3–quart, or larger, slow cooker as it browns.

ADD the onion and bell pepper to the pan and sauté over medium-high heat until browned, about 4 minutes. Add the fresh chile peppers and garlic and cook for another 30 seconds. Stir in the cumin, oregano, and flour until dispersed evenly. Stir in the broth and tomatoes and continue stirring until simmering and slightly thickened.

ADD the mixture to the beef and stir. Cover the cooker and cook for 4 to 5 hours on high, or 8 to 9 hours on low, until the beef is fork-tender. Stir in the ground chiles and cook on high for 15 minutes. Serve with hot rice or wedges of cornbread, if desired.

what else?

- Feel free to serve with refried beans, or simmered kidney beans, if desired.

- Sirloin gives you the leanest chili and very tender meat, but if you want a richer taste, use chuck.

Bistro Beef Stew

Like the chocolate chip cookie, bistro stews are so down-to-earth, so unpretentious, and so damn good that they transcend the ordinary, climbing to the upper "statusphere" with every mouthful. Although this recipe is constructed like any stew, its sophistication comes from the broth (all wine) and the pronounced fragrance of herbs (an entire bunch of thyme). Like all stews, this one gets better with age, so when possible, plan to cook it a day or two before serving.

SERVINGS

PRECOOK

20 minutes

SLOW COOK

3 to 4 hours on high, or 6 to 8 hours on low, in a 5- to 6-quart slow cooker

AT THE END

5 minutes

⅓	cup flour
1	teaspoon kosher salt
¼	teaspoon ground black pepper
2	pounds trimmed beef chuck, cut into 1½-inch cubes
2 to 3	tablespoons olive oil, divided
2	strips bacon, cut into ½-inch pieces
2	medium onions, cut into ½-inch dice
1	large carrot, peeled and cut into ¼-inch-thick slices

1	celery rib, cut into ¼-inch-thick slices
5	cloves garlic, coarsely chopped
2	cups dry red wine, such as Cabernet Sauvignon
1	small bunch (about 1 ounce) fresh thyme, tied with kitchen string
1	tablespoon finely grated orange zest
2	tablespoons chopped fresh Italian (flat-leaf) parsley

COMBINE the flour, salt, and pepper in a mixing bowl. Add the beef cubes and toss to coat evenly with flour; pat off the excess flour and reserve the seasoned flour mixture.

HEAT 1 tablespoon olive oil in a large deep skillet over medium-high heat. Brown the beef in 2 to 3 batches, about 3 minutes per side, adding more oil with each batch, as needed. Transfer each batch of meat to a 5- to 6-quart slow cooker after it is browned.

REDUCE the heat to medium, add the bacon, and cook until crisp. Add the onions, carrot, and celery and sauté until browned, about 5 minutes. Add the garlic and cook for another minute, stirring constantly. Add the reserved seasoned flour and stir until browned, about 2 minutes. Add the wine and heat to boiling. Pour the mixture over the beef in the slow cooker. Bury the bunch of thyme in the center of the cooker. Cover and cook for 3 to 4 hours on high,or 6 to 8 hours on low, until the beef and vegetables are fork-tender.

REMOVE the thyme. Stir in the orange zest and parsley and cook for 5 minutes on high. Serve with lots of crusty bread, if desired, for mopping up the gravy.

what else?

- Although beef chuck is my preferred cut for stew, generic beef cubes are fine for this recipe.

cooking with wine

There are two rules for cooking with wine:

1. Never use a great wine in stew (think about it; it would be like adding garlic, tomato, and thyme to a glass of great Bordeaux).

2. Be careful of slow cooking with very dry wines, such as red wines from Burgundy. Tannins, the astringent chemicals that give these wines a drying effect on the tongue, indicate good potential for a wine's longevity. But they tend to turn bitter in cooking, especially when simmering for many hours in a slow cooker.

Barbecue Pork and Beans

Pork and beans is usually more beans than pork; not so here. This hearty stew is overrun with melt-in-your-mouth barbecued pork, laced with just enough beans to sop up the sauce. I suggest you use pork shoulder and cut it into cubes yourself, even if precut pork is available. Generic meat cubes can come from anywhere on the pig, and the richly marbled, well-exercised shoulder meat is what you want here. On the other hand, any type of dried beans will be fine. I usually use a white bean (pea bean, navy, Great Northern, white kidney, or butter beans), but you can use pintos or pink beans. I even tried a bag of mixed beans in this recipe, and it was delicious.

1   cup (about ½ pound) dried beans, such as a white bean, pinto, kidney, or a mixture

2   pounds boneless pork shoulder, trimmed of fat and cut into 1-inch cubes

3   teaspoons Southwest-style spice rub, home-made (page 68) or purchased, divided

2   slices bacon, finely chopped

1   medium onion, cut into ½-inch chunks

2   carrots, peeled and cut into ½-inch chunks

1   celery rib, cut into ½-inch-thick slices

1   teaspoon ground cumin, preferably ground from whole seeds toasted in a dry skillet

1   tablespoon flour

3   cups chicken broth

½   cup barbecue sauce, homemade (page 69) or purchased

1   can (about 15 ounces) diced tomatoes, with their juice

SERVINGS

PRECOOK

1 hour to overnight (depending on how you soak the beans)

SLOW COOK

8 to 10 hours on low in a 5- to 6-quart slow cooker

PUT the beans in a bowl, cover with at least 3 inches of water, and soak overnight. Or put the beans in a saucepan, cover with 3 inches of water, and bring to a boil. Continue boiling for 3 minutes, remove from the heat, and soak the beans for 1 hour. Drain.

WHILE THE BEANS ARE SOAKING, rub the pork cubes with 2 teaspoons of the spice rub; wrap well and refrigerate.

COOK the bacon in a large deep skillet, prefer-ably cast-iron, over medium heat until most of the fat has rendered and coats the bottom of the skillet, about 5 minutes. Remove the cooked bacon and reserve.

Turn the heat up to medium-high and brown the pork in the bacon fat, in batches if needed; trans-fer to a 5- to 6-quart slow cooker. Add the beans and the bacon, and toss to combine.

ADD the onion, carrots, and celery to the skillet and sauté until tender and lightly browned, about 4 minutes, stirring often. Stir in the cumin, the remaining teaspoon of spice rub, and the flour and stir to coat the vegetables. Add the chicken broth and simmer until slightly thickened, stirring often. Stir in the barbecue sauce and tomatoes and pour into the slow cooker. Stir to combine, cover the cooker, and cook for 8 to 10 hours on low, until the beans are tender. Stir and serve.

southwest-style spice rub

Makes ½ cup

1   tablespoon kosher salt

2   tablespoons paprika

¼   cup light brown sugar

1   teaspoon ancho chile powder

1   teaspoon chipotle chile powder

½   teaspoon ground cumin, preferably
    ground from whole seeds toasted in a
    dry skillet

½   teaspoon ground black pepper

MIX all the ingredients together and store in a tightly sealed container at room temperature for up to 1 month.

all-purpose barbecue sauce

Makes about 1 cup

⅓   **cup ketchup**

3   **tablespoons brown mustard**

3   **tablespoons apple cider vinegar**

3   **tablespoons light brown sugar**

1   **tablespoon Tabasco hot pepper sauce**

½   **teaspoon ground black pepper**

MIX all the ingredients together to blend. Store in the refrigerator in a tightly closed container for up to 2 weeks.

Tunisian Lamb Tagine with Toasted Almonds and Couscous

The stews of North Africa are known as *tagines* (also spelled *tajines*), after the conical ceramic vessel in which they are traditionally made. The lid of a tagine is tall, causing the steam coming off of the stew to cool at its upper reaches and precipitate back into the vessel, so that none of the aroma or flavor is lost during cooking. This is exactly what happens in a slow cooker. The flavors in this tagine are classic Berber: cumin, coriander, cinnamon, and pepper, which have been cultivated for thousands of years by these ancient peoples in the mountain and desert regions of Morocco, Algeria, and Tunisia. Ground toasted almonds thicken the broth in the last minutes of cooking. The tagine is traditionally served with couscous.

2	pounds lamb cubes for stew	½	teaspoon ground allspice
	Kosher salt	1½	cups beef broth
4	tablespoons extra-virgin olive oil, divided	1	can (about 15 ounces) diced tomatoes, with their juice
1	pound parsnips (about 5), peeled and cut into 1-inch chunks	1	teaspoon coarsely ground black pepper
2	large sweet potatoes, peeled and cut into 1½-inch chunks	1	cinnamon stick, about 3 inches
2	celery ribs, cut into 1-inch-thick slices	1	dried red chile pepper
2	onions, cut into 1-inch cubes	¼	cup ground toasted almonds (see page 73)
4	cloves garlic, minced		Juice and finely grated zest of ½ lemon
1	tablespoon ground cumin, preferably ground from whole seeds toasted in a dry skillet	2½	cups water
		2	cups couscous
1	tablespoon ground coriander	¼	cup chopped fresh Italian (flat-leaf) parsley or fresh cilantro, or a mixture of the two

SEASON the lamb liberally with salt to taste. Heat 2 tablespoons of the olive oil in a large skillet over medium-high heat and brown the lamb lightly in batches, 3 to 5 minutes per side. Transfer each batch to a 5- to 6-quart slow cooker after it is browned.

ADD another tablespoon olive oil to the skillet. Add the parsnips, sweet potatoes, celery, and onions and sauté until lightly browned and barely tender, about 4 minutes. Stir in the garlic, cumin, coriander, and allspice, and cook until the vegetables are coated and the spices are aromatic, about 1 minute. Transfer to the cooker.

ADD the beef broth to the skillet and heat to boiling, scraping up any browned bits clinging to the bottom of the pan; pour into the cooker.

SERVINGS

PRECOOK

20 minutes

SLOW COOK

3 to 4 hours on high, or 6 to 8 hours on low, in a 5- to 6-quart slow cooker

AT THE END

15 minutes

CONTINUED

Tunisian Lamb Tagine with
Toasted Almonds and Couscous CONTINUED

ADD the tomatoes to the cooker, and stir gently to combine. Add the black pepper, cinnamon stick, and chile pepper, submerging the cinnamon and chile. Cover the cooker and cook for 3 to 4 hours on high, or 6 to 8 hours on low, until fork-tender.

WHILE THE STEW IS COOKING, mix the almonds, lemon juice, and lemon zest in a small bowl.

WHEN THE STEW IS DONE, remove the cinnamon stick and chile pepper. Stir in the almond mixture and cook on high until slightly thickened, about 15 minutes. At the same time, bring the remaining 1 tablespoon olive oil and the water to a boil in a large saucepan. Stir in the couscous until fully moistened, cover, remove from the heat, and let rest for 5 minutes.

SERVE the stew on a bed of couscous and sprinkle with chopped parsley and/or cilantro.

what else?

- For chicken tagine, substitute boneless chicken thighs for the lamb and eliminate the allspice.

- Tagines can also be served on any small pasta, such as orzo or acini de pepe, cooked according to the package directions, or with toasted couscous (a.k.a. Israeli couscous, pearl couscous, or super couscous). To make toasted couscous: Heat 1 tablespoon olive oil in a large saucepan over medium-high heat. Add 2 cups couscous and sauté until lightly toasted, about 3 minutes. Add 3 ¾ cups boiling water and salt and pepper to taste. Reduce the heat to medium, cover, and simmer until the liquid is absorbed, about 12 minutes.

toasting nuts

To toast nuts, heat a heavy skillet over medium-high heat for 3 minutes. Add the nuts, stir for 30 seconds, and remove from the heat. Continue stirring until the nuts are lightly toasted and very aromatic. Below are suggested times for toasting various nuts. Remember that only 30 seconds of that time are over the heat.

NUT	TOASTING TIME
Almonds, whole, blanched, or skin-on	4 minutes
Almonds, sliced or slivered	3 minutes
Almonds, chopped or ground	1 minute
Cashews, whole or halves	4 minutes
Hazelnuts, whole or halves, blanched	4 minutes
Hazelnuts, chopped or ground	3 minutes
Pecans, halves or pieces	3 minutes
Pecans, chopped or ground	1 minute
Pine nuts	1 minute
Pistachio nuts	2 minutes
Walnuts, halves or pieces	3 minutes
Walnuts, chopped or ground	1 minute

Lemony Veal Stew
with Chickpeas and Spinach

Stews are so central to cold-weather cooking that we forget some are as bright and fresh as spring. The spare, clean quality of veal lends itself to this light type of stew, flavored with lemon, thyme, and rosemary. Fresh spinach leaves are stirred in at the end; the heat of the stew is enough to cook them through in a few minutes.

SERVINGS

PRECOOK

20 minutes

SLOW COOK

3 to 4 hours on high, or 6 to 8 hours on low, in a 5- to 6-quart slow cooker

AT THE END

2 minutes

½	cup flour
1	teaspoon kosher salt
½	teaspoon coarsely ground black pepper
3	pounds boneless veal shoulder, cut into 1½-inch cubes for stew
¼	cup extra-virgin olive oil, divided
1	medium onion, cut into ½-inch dice
1	celery rib, cut into ½-inch dice
3	cloves garlic, minced
1	teaspoon chopped fresh rosemary leaves

1	teaspoon dried thyme
¼	teaspoon ground ginger
½	cup dry white wine
1½	cups chicken broth
1	can (about 15 ounces) chickpeas, drained and rinsed
	Juice and finely grated zest of ½ lemon
1	bay leaf
1	bag (6 ounces) baby spinach, coarsely chopped (about 6 cups)

MIX the flour, salt, and pepper in a medium-large mixing bowl. Add the veal and toss until the meat is evenly coated; pat off the excess flour and reserve the seasoned flour mixture.

HEAT half the olive oil in a large, deep skillet over medium-high heat. Add the veal in batches and brown lightly on all sides. Transfer each batch to a 5- to 6-quart slow cooker after it is browned.

ADD the rest of the oil to the skillet. Add the onion and celery and sauté over medium heat until tender, but not browned, about 3 minutes. Add the garlic, rosemary, thyme, and ginger and stir once or twice. Add the reserved seasoned flour, stirring until the vegetables are well coated. Stir in the wine and bring to a boil. Add the broth, return to a boil, and stir until slightly thickened. Pour over the veal. Add the chickpeas, lemon juice, lemon zest, and bay leaf to the cooker and stir to combine. Cover the cooker and cook for 3 to 4 hours on high, or 6 to 8 hours on low, until the meat is fork-tender. Remove the bay leaf.

STIR in the spinach and cook for 1 to 2 minutes, until the spinach is wilted. Serve immediately.

what else?

- You can increase the lemony character of this stew by using lemon thyme in place of regular thyme.

- Although veal shoulder will hold up to long cooking, the leanness and tenderness of veal means you will get moister results if you stop the cooking near the low end of the time range. Use grass-fed veal instead of formula-fed if you know you are going to cook it longer.

Marrakech Chicken Stew with Preserved Lemon and Olives

This pungent, fragrant chicken stew is not for the weak of palate. Radiating the aromas of toasted cumin and coriander, and spiked with the salty-sour pucker of cured lemons and olives, it produces a heady and exotic effect. If you can't find preserved lemons in your local food markets (high-end stores usually stock them), you can order them or make them yourself. Internet sources and a recipe follow on pages 78 and 79, respectively.

1	tablespoon cumin seed		2	cloves garlic, minced
2	teaspoons coriander seed		½	cup white wine
½	cup flour		1½	cups chicken broth
1	teaspoon salt			Juice and finely grated zest of 1 lemon
1	teaspoon ground black pepper		1	preserved lemon, homemade (page 79) or purchased (see What Else? on page 78), finely chopped
4	pounds chicken pieces, or 1 cut-up chicken, skin removed			
2	tablespoons extra-virgin olive oil		¼	cup chopped fresh Italian (flat-leaf) parsley
2	onions, chopped		½	cup pitted kalamata olives

HEAT a medium skillet, preferably cast-iron, over medium-high heat. Add the cumin seed and stir until aromatic, about 30 seconds. Turn off the heat, add the coriander seed, and stir for 30 seconds. Scrape the spices into a mortar with a pestle or into a spice grinder and grind until the cumin and coriander are coarsely ground. Mix with the flour, salt, and pepper in a medium-large mixing bowl and dredge the chicken pieces in the seasoned flour mixture; pat off the excess flour and reserve the mixture.

HEAT the oil in an extra-large skillet over medium-high heat; brown the chicken pieces on both sides, in batches, about 3 minutes per side, then transfer to a 5- to 6-quart slow cooker.

REDUCE the heat under the skillet to medium. Add the onions and sauté until tender, about 2 minutes. Add the garlic and the reserved seasoned flour mixture and stir until the flour is lightly toasted, about 3 minutes. Add the wine and chicken broth and stir until the sauce is slightly thickened. Remove from the heat and stir in the lemon zest (but not the juice).

CONTINUED

SERVINGS

PRECOOK

20 minutes

SLOW COOK

2 to 3 hours on high, or 4 to 6 hours on low, in a 5- to 6-quart slow cooker

Marrakech Chicken Stew
with Preserved Lemon and Olives CONTINUED

POUR over the chicken and scatter the chopped preserved lemon over the top. Cover the cooker and cook for 2 to 3 hours on high, or 4 to 6 hours on low, until an instant-read thermometer inserted into the thickest part of one of the uppermost pieces of chicken registers 170°F. Keep warm for as long as 4 hours.

REMOVE the chicken to a platter. Stir the lemon juice, parsley, and olives into the sauce, and spoon over the chicken.

what else?

- If you can't find preserved lemons at your neighborhood grocery store, you can order them from Mustapha's Moroccan (www.mustaphas.com) or Zamouri Spices (www.zamourispices.com), or you can make them yourself (see facing page).

preserved lemons

Makes 2 cups

**4 or 5 lemons (depending on size),
scrubbed clean**

Kosher salt

Fresh lemon juice, as needed

CUT the tips off the ends of the lemons. Cut into quarters lengthwise, leaving them attached at one end. Pack the lemons with as much salt as they will hold.

PLACE the lemons in a wide-mouth quart-size jar, packing them in as tightly as possible. As you push the lemons into the jar, some juice will be squeezed from them.

WHEN THE JAR IS FULL, the juice should cover the lemons; if it doesn't, add some fresh lemon juice.

SEAL the jar and set aside for 3 to 4 weeks at room temperature, shaking the jar every day to keep the salt well distributed, until the lemon rinds are soft. The lemons should be covered with juice at all times; add more as needed.

RINSE before using.

what else?

- If you can't wait the 3 to 4 weeks it takes to preserve lemons, you can make a respectable facsimile by cutting however many lemons you want to preserve into ¼-inch-thick slices. Sprinkle the slices generously with kosher salt on both sides, and set aside for 1 hour. Rinse before using.

Seafood Caldo with Chorizo

Caldos are the hearty, chunky soups of Portugal and Spain. This one takes the flavors of the region and ups the ante of ingredients into the realm of stew. Although the flavors are multilayered and complex, they are not challenging, and the spice level is determined completely by the type of chorizo you use. Even if you like your food on the fiery side, I suggest using a mild chorizo. Pepper has a tendency to grow hotter during slow cooking, and you can always add a pinch of crushed pepper flakes at the end. As with all seafood stews and soups, you can make the broth any time, but add your fish no more than 20 minutes before serving.

1	cup dry white wine
1	cup water
18	littleneck clams, cleaned (clams should be tightly closed)
	Pinch of saffron threads
1	tablespoon extra-virgin olive oil
8	ounces fresh chorizo (preferably mild), cut into ½-inch-thick slices
1	medium onion, chopped
1	red or green bell pepper, stemmed, seeded, and cut into ½-inch dice
2	celery ribs, halved lengthwise and cut into thin slices
4	cloves garlic, minced, divided
1	cup canned diced tomatoes, with their juice
1	bay leaf
½	teaspoon dried thyme
1	teaspoon sweet paprika
½	teaspoon kosher salt
¼	teaspoon ground black pepper
	Juice and finely grated zest of ½ lemon
3	tablespoons chopped fresh Italian (flat-leaf) parsley
2	tablespoons coarsely chopped toasted almonds (see page 73)
8	ounces salmon fillet, skin removed, bones removed, and cut into 1-inch pieces
8	ounces jumbo shrimp (15 to 20 count), shelled and cleaned

SERVINGS

PRECOOK

20 minutes

SLOW COOK

3 to 4 hours on high, or 6 to 8 hours on low, in a 5- to 6-quart slow cooker

AT THE END

20 minutes

BRING the wine and water to a boil in a large deep skillet with a tight-fitting lid over high heat. Add the clams, cover, and boil until the clams open, 4 to 8 minutes, removing the clams to a bowl with a slotted spoon as soon as they open. Discard any unopened clams. Strain the cooking liquid through a dampened coffee filter or several layers of damp cheesecloth to remove grit. You should have about 2 cups; add more water if you have less. Add the saffron to the liquid and set aside. Store the clams in the refrigerator while the stew cooks.

HEAT the oil in a large deep skillet over medium-high heat. Brown the chorizo slices on both sides, about 2 minutes per side. Transfer to a 5- to 6-quart slow cooker.

CONTINUED

ADD the onion, bell pepper, and celery and sauté until tender and lightly browned, about 3 minutes. Add three-quarters of the garlic and sauté for another 30 seconds. Add the reserved clam cooking liquid, the diced tomatoes, bay leaf, thyme, paprika, salt, and pepper and bring to a simmer. Pour into the slow cooker, cover the cooker, and cook for 3 to 4 hours on high, or 6 to 8 hours on low.

MEANWHILE, mix together the remaining garlic, lemon juice and zest, parsley, and almonds; set aside.

ABOUT 30 MINUTES BEFORE SERVING, remove the clams from the refrigerator and turn the slow cooker to high. Add the salmon and shrimp to the slow cooker, push gently to submerge, and cook until the fish flakes when pressed gently, about 20 minutes. Remove the bay leaf.

TO SERVE, place 3 clams in each of 6 large soup bowls. Ladle the caldo over the clams and sprinkle with some of the parsley mixture; serve immediately.

what else?

- Alter the seafood to take advantage of whatever looks brightest and is most readily available to you. Just try to have a mixture of shellfish and fish.

Duck with Red Wine, Wild Mushrooms, and Forest Herbs

We picture duck with a crackling skin and mahogany glaze so often that we forget its rich dark meat also makes a great stew. This recipe complements the opulent quality of duck with a fruit-filled red wine (like Cabernet or Merlot), two kinds of exotic mushrooms (dried wild and fresh cremini), and a bouquet of rosemary and thyme, with their fragrance of pine trees and forest shrubs. The challenge of any duck recipe is getting rid of the fat. The easiest way to do this is to remove all the skin and as much of the fat as you can see before you start cooking. Then instead of adding oil for browning the duck and vegetables, you gently cook some of the duck skin in a dry skillet until its fat is rendered, so it becomes the only fat in the stew.

1	cup beef broth
½	cup dried wild mushrooms, any type
1	duck (about 5 pounds), cut into 2 breast halves, 2 thighs, 2 drumsticks, and 2 wings
¼	cup flour
1	teaspoon kosher salt
1	teaspoon ground black pepper
	Pinch of ground cloves
1	large onion, cut into ½-inch dice
1	large carrot, peeled and cut into ½-inch dice
1	large celery rib, cut into ½-inch dice
12	large cremini mushrooms, cut into ¼-inch-thick slices
2	teaspoons chopped fresh rosemary
1	teaspoon fresh thyme leaves
1	cup dry, fruity red wine, such as Cabernet Sauvignon or Merlot
1	cup canned diced tomato, drained
2	tablespoons chopped fresh Italian (flat-leaf) parsley

SERVINGS

PRECOOK

30 minutes

SLOW COOK

2 to 3 hours on high, or 4 to 6 hours on low, in a 5- to 6-quart slow cooker

BRING the broth to a boil in a small saucepan. Add the dried mushrooms, remove from the heat, and set aside for 10 minutes, until the mushrooms are plump and moist.

REMOVE the skin and visible fat from the duck pieces, reserving half and discarding the rest. Cut the breast pieces in half. Heat a large deep skillet, preferably cast-iron, over medium heat. Add the reserved duck skin and fat and cook until there is ¼ inch of melted duck fat in the pan. Remove the remaining skin and solid fat pieces and discard.

MIX the flour, salt, pepper, and cloves in a medium-large mixing bowl. Add the duck pieces and toss to coat; pat off the excess flour and reserve the spiced flour mixture.

PLACE the skillet containing the duck fat over medium-high heat. Brown the floured duck pieces on both sides, about 4 minutes per side. Transfer to a 5- to 6-quart slow cooker.

CONTINUED

Duck with Red Wine, Wild Mushrooms, and Forest Herbs CONTINUED

ADD the onion, carrot, celery, and cremini mushrooms to the pan and sauté until lightly browned, about 4 minutes. Add the reserved seasoned flour and stir until the vegetables are coated. Add the rosemary, thyme, and wine and bring to a boil. Add the soaked mushrooms and their soaking liquid and the tomatoes, bring to a simmer, and stir until the sauce is slightly thickened.

POUR over the duck and toss gently to coat. Cover the slow cooker and cook for 2 to 3 hours on high, or 4 to 6 hours on low, until the duck is very tender. Sprinkle with the parsley and serve.

Beef Stew Provençal

The flavor of Provence is all in the herbs—anise, fennel, thyme, lavender, and rosemary—and, of course, the garlic, lots of garlic. This straightforward beef stew is brought to life with those ingredients. You are familiar with the drill: flour and season the beef, brown it, brown some vegetables, add broth, and simmer till it's done. But what a difference the nod to Provence makes. Your idea of beef stew will be forever transformed.

½	cup flour
1	teaspoon kosher salt
¼	teaspoon ground black pepper
1	teaspoon ground aniseed
2	teaspoons dried herbes de Provence
2½	pounds trimmed beef chuck, cut into 1½-inch cubes
3 to 4	tablespoons olive oil, divided
1	large onion, cut into ½-inch dice
1	bulb fennel, leaves and tough stems trimmed, cut into ½-inch-thick slices
1	whole head garlic, separated into cloves, each peeled and halved
2	teaspoons chopped fresh rosemary leaves
½	cup dry red wine
½	cup orange juice
1	cup beef broth
1	cup canned crushed tomatoes
3	whole star anise
¼	cup coarsely chopped pitted black olives, preferably niçoise
2	tablespoon chopped fresh Italian (flat-leaf) parsley

SERVINGS

PRECOOK

30 minutes

SLOW COOK

3 to 4 hours on high, or 6 to 8 hours on low, in a 5- to 6-quart slow cooker

COMBINE the flour, salt, pepper, aniseed, and herbes de Provence in a medium-large mixing bowl. Add the beef cubes and toss to coat evenly with flour; pat off the excess flour and reserve the flour mixture.

HEAT 1 tablespoon olive oil in a large deep skillet, preferably cast-iron, over medium-high heat. Brown the beef on all sides in 2 to 3 batches, about 6 minutes for each batch, adding another tablespoon olive oil with each one. After each batch is browned, transfer to a 5- to 6-quart slow cooker.

REDUCE heat to medium, and add the remaining 1 tablespoon olive oil to the pan. Add the onion, fennel, and garlic, and sauté until browned, about 5 minutes. Add the reserved seasoned

CONTINUED

Beef Stew Provençal CONTINUED

flour and stir until browned, about 3 minutes. Add the rosemary, wine, orange juice, broth, and tomatoes, and heat, stirring until the sauce is thickened.

POUR over the beef in the slow cooker and drop the star anise into the pot. Cover the cooker and cook for 3 to 4 hours on high, or 6 to 8 hours on low, until the beef and vegetables are fork-tender. Remove the star anise. Stir in the olives and parsley and serve.

what else?

- Herbes de Provence is an herb mixture that is sold along with other dried herbs. It usually contains basil, fennel, lavender, marjoram, rosemary, sage, savory, and thyme.

- This stew is also delicious made with lamb.

Slow Cooker Braising

ANYONE WHO COOKS KNOWS HOW TO BRAISE, but very few can tell you how they do it. Braising is a mystery, not because it's tricky, but simply because most cooks don't know what it means.

The confusion stems from braising's dual nature. Braising is a composite cooking technique. First the ingredient is browned, either by sautéing, broiling, or grilling, and then it is simmered until it is cooked through. The initial step creates flavor, and the simmering step ensures tender, melt-in-your-mouth results.

Of all the traditional cooking techniques, braising is best suited to slow cooking. Anyone who has used a slow cooker is familiar with the method, for it is how almost all slow-cooked meals are prepared.

Braising in a slow cooker is nearly identical to stove-top braising; the only difference is that you do not need to use nearly as much liquid for simmering. Typically, ¼ cup of liquid per serving is sufficient. Although this seems skimpy when you load up the cooker, you will find that plenty of sauce will develop as juices from the meats and vegetables mingle with the cooking liquid.

I can't overemphasize the importance of browning for flavoring a braised dish. A browned surface, especially when cooking with meat, is the very essence of succulence. Season your ingredients well and use a skillet that's big enough to hold your ingredients without crowding. The skillet should be heavy, and preferably not nonstick (I usually use a large, heavy cast-iron skillet). Season your ingredients well, and heat the pan for several minutes before adding anything. When you add a thin film of oil, it should begin to smoke across the bottom of the pan on contact. Add your ingredients, making sure there is lots of space around them, and then don't touch for at least 3 minutes, until you see a hint of crust creeping up the sides of the searing food. Brown ingredients all over—top, bottom, and sides (if they're thick enough)—and as soon as a gorgeous brown crust develops, transfer everything to the slow cooker.

Once you turn on the cooker, you won't have anything else to do until dinnertime, so for the sake of succulence, pay attention when browning. Your taste buds will thank you.

Recipes

Slow-Cooked Teriyaki Chicken

In Japanese, *teri* literally means "gloss" or "sheen" and refers to the lustrous lacquer that glazes broiled (*yaki*) foods. In American parlance, *teriyaki* has come to connote the sauce that creates the shine, traditionally a mixture of soy sauce, sugar, and sweet wine. In this easy slow-cooked teriyaki, chicken thighs are permeated with pungency. Slowly simmered in the sauce, they are then crisped under a broiler and painted with the thickened glaze. By using skinless chicken, you cut the fat content in half, and the sweet fermented flavor of the teriyaki comes through in every bite. Serve with boiled rice, if desired.

4-6

SERVINGS

PRECOOK

15 minutes

SLOW COOK

2 to 3 hours on high in a 5- to 6-quart slow cooker

AT THE END

5 minutes

1   tablespoon vegetable oil

4   pounds skinless chicken thighs (about 8), bone-in

2   cloves garlic, minced

1   tablespoon finely grated gingerroot

¼   cup plus 1½ tablespoons water

⅓   cup soy sauce

¼   cup sherry or apple juice

1   tablespoon rice wine vinegar

2   tablespoons dark molasses

3   tablespoons honey

2   teaspoons cornstarch

1   teaspoon dark sesame oil

2   scallions, trimmed and cut into thin slices

HEAT the oil in a large skillet over high heat. Brown the chicken thighs in batches on both sides, about 3 minutes per side, then transfer to a 5- to 6-quart slow cooker.

ADD the garlic and ginger to the skillet and cook over medium-high heat until aromatic, about 30 seconds. Add the ¼ cup water and scrape up any browned bits stuck to the bottom of the skillet. Add the soy sauce, sherry, rice wine vinegar, molasses, and honey and stir to blend. Pour over the chicken, cover the cooker, and cook on high for 2 to 3 hours, until the chicken is cooked through.

PREHEAT a broiler to high; remove the chicken to a broiler tray and broil for 2 minutes on each side. While the chicken is broiling, pour the liquid from the cooker into a skillet. Bring to a boil over medium-high heat. Dissolve the cornstarch in the 1½ tablespoons of water, add to the sauce in the skillet, and stir until the sauce is lightly thickened, about 1 minute. Arrange the chicken on a serving platter and spoon the sauce over top. Drizzle with sesame oil, and sprinkle with the scallions.

what else?

- If you are not a fan of dark-meat chicken, you can prepare this recipe with chicken breast, but only cook it on high, and stop the cooking after about 2 hours, as soon as the meat registers 165°F on a meat thermometer. Then broil as directed in the recipe.

- If you like your teriyaki spicy, replace the sesame oil with chili oil.

Sausage and Tomato Ragù with Pasta

When Italian Americans refer to a tomato-meat sauce as "gravy," this ragù is what they're talking about. Brimming with sausage, wine, and meat broth, it is a sauce distilled from meat—cooked so slowly that the essences of meat and tomato literally merge. To the uninitiated, conditioned by commercial pasta sauces to believe that meat sauce is just tomato sauce flavored with meat, this brush with authenticity is a revelation. Try it at your own risk; you may never be able to go back to jarred meat sauce again.

2	tablespoons extra-virgin olive oil
2	pounds mild Italian sausage, cut into 2-inch lengths
2	medium onions, cut into ½-inch dice
2	celery ribs, cut into ½-inch-thick slices
2	large carrots, peeled and cut into ½-inch dice
4	cloves garlic, finely chopped
1	tablespoon fresh rosemary leaves
	Pinch of ground allspice
1	teaspoon kosher salt
½	teaspoon coarsely ground black pepper
¼	cup flour
1	cup dry red wine
2	cups chicken broth or beef broth
1	can (about 28 ounces) crushed tomatoes
1	can (about 15 ounces) tomato sauce
1	pound short pasta, such as penne, ziti, or rigatoni

HEAT the oil in a large deep skillet over medium-high heat. Brown the sausage on all sides, about 2 minutes per side, then transfer to a 5- to 6-quart slow cooker.

ADD the onions, celery, and carrots to the oil remaining in the skillet and sauté until lightly browned, about 4 minutes. Add the garlic, rosemary, allspice, salt, and pepper and cook for another 30 seconds. Add the flour and stir until incorporated. Add the wine and bring to a boil. Add the broth, crushed tomatoes, and tomato sauce and stir to incorporate, scraping up any browned bits from the bottom of the pan to blend them with the sauce. Heat to simmering and pour over the sausages. Cover the cooker and cook for 4 to 5 hours on high, or 8 to 10 hours on low.

COOK the pasta in rapidly boiling, lightly salted water until tender, about 10 minutes; drain and serve with the ragù.

SERVINGS

(1½ quarts sauce)

PRECOOK
15 minutes

SLOW COOK
4 to 5 hours on high, or 8 to 10 hours on low, in a 5- to 6-quart slow cooker

AT THE END
10 minutes

CONTINUED

Sausage and Tomato Ragù with Pasta CONTINUED

what else?

- If you like your sauce spicy, replace half the sausage with hot Italian sausage or add a pinch of red pepper flakes with the salt and pepper.

- You can replace half the sausage with ground meat (beef, veal, pork, or a combination) for a thicker sauce.

- This sauce is great rewarmed, and it freezes well.

Slow-Cooked South Carolina Pulled Pork

In South Carolina, where pork is considered the only meat, the shoulder (a.k.a. butt, which is actually the upper shoulder) or picnic (the lower shoulder or arm) is usually slow-cooked until it collapses into a mass of juicy, fatty, succulent shreds. This piece of nirvana is traditionally created over a low, smoky wood fire, lovingly tended to for the 8 to 10 hours that it takes the pig to transsubstantiate into pulled pork. But if you don't have a barbecue pit or the time to minister to the beast, a slow cooker is a great option. The pork will be as tender and juicy as the real thing; all that you'll miss is the smoke.

1 tablespoon onion salt	2 tablespoons vegetable oil
2 tablespoons sweet Hungarian paprika	¾ cup apple cider vinegar
4 tablespoons light brown sugar	2 teaspoons Tabasco sauce
2 teaspoons chili powder	6 large soft rolls (optional)
½ teaspoon ground allspice	1½ cups coleslaw (optional)
½ teaspoon ground black pepper	
3 pounds boneless pork shoulder (picnic) or boneless country-style pork ribs	

MIX the onion salt, paprika, 1 tablespoon of the brown sugar, the chili powder, allspice, and black pepper in a medium mixing bowl. Remove 1 tablespoon of the spice mix and reserve; rub the remainder all over the pork. Wrap the pork in plastic wrap and set aside for 1 hour, or refrigerate overnight.

HEAT the oil in a large skillet over medium-high heat. Brown the pork on all sides, about 4 minutes per side, and transfer to a 4–quart, or larger, slow cooker. Add the vinegar, reserved spice mixture, and the remaining 3 tablespoons of brown sugar to the skillet and bring to a boil, scraping up any browned bits from the bottom of the pan. Pour over the pork, cover the cooker, and cook for 6 to 10 hours on low, until the pork is fork-tender.

TO SERVE, remove the pork from the cooker, cut into ½-inch-thick slices, and shred the slices into bite-size pieces with two forks. Add the Tabasco to the liquid in the cooker. Return the pork to the cooker and toss to coat with liquid. Serve immediately, or keep warm for up to several hours. Serve on soft rolls with coleslaw, if desired.

6

SERVINGS

PRECOOK
1 hour to overnight

SLOW COOK
6 to 10 hours on low in a 4-quart, or larger, slow cooker

AT THE END
10 minutes

Braised Sweet-and-Sour Brisket

My mother didn't cook much, but she made a glorious brisket. This is her recipe, reconfigured for a slow cooker, which simply means a little less liquid, a lot more time, and incredibly tender results—something my mother was never able to guarantee. The brisket comes from the breast of a cow, and there are two cuts. The first cut (a.k.a. flat cut) is leaner and has a more regular grain, making it easier to slice. The second cut (a.k.a. deckle or point) is thicker, triangular, and striated with more fat, which makes the meat juicier but harder to cut into uniform slices. Either one will be delicious in this recipe, but you will get a better yield and nicer results using a first-cut brisket.

SERVINGS

PRECOOK

20 minutes

SLOW COOK

4 to 6 hours on high, or 8 to 10 hours on low, in a 5- to 6-quart slow cooker

3	pounds beef brisket, trimmed of excess fat		4	celery ribs, cut into ½-inch-thick slices
	Kosher salt		4	cloves garlic, minced
	Coarsely ground black pepper		6	tablespoons cider vinegar
2	tablespoons vegetable oil, divided		¼	cup dark brown sugar
2	large onions, chopped		½	cup ketchup
6	carrots, peeled and cut into 1-inch lengths		1½	cups beef broth

SEASON the brisket liberally with salt and pepper to taste. Heat 1 tablespoon of the oil in a large skillet over medium-high heat. Brown the brisket on both sides, about 5 minutes per side, starting fatty side down. Transfer to a 5- to 6-quart slow cooker.

ADD another tablespoon of oil to the skillet. Add the onions, carrots, and celery and cook until browned, about 5 minutes. Add the garlic, and cook for 30 seconds. Add the vinegar, brown sugar, ketchup, and broth and bring to a boil. Pour over the brisket, cover the cooker, and cook 4 to 6 hours on high, or 8 to 10 hours on low, until the meat is very tender.

CONTINUED

Braised Sweet-and-Sour Brisket CONTINUED

TRANSFER the brisket to a cutting board and skim the fat from the surface of the juices. Cut the brisket across its grain in ¼-inch-thick slices and arrange so they are overlapping on a large platter. Surround with vegetables and spoon enough sauce over the top to moisten; serve the remaining sauce on the side.

what else?

- You can cook beef chuck in the same way as brisket.

- Fruit is a popular addition to sweet-and-sour brisket. Add 12 to 15 dried apricots or prunes to the slow cooker along with the sauce, and replace ½ cup of the beef broth with wine or fruit juice.

1/20/13 — made w/ pork
~8 hrs = dry meat due t
lack of fat. GREAT flavor!

Thai Short Ribs

Short ribs, the tough, flavorful, fatty cuts from the ends of the rib bones, come two ways: short sections of individual ribs (English cut) or long strips cut across several ribs (flanken cut). For this recipe you will need the more compact English cut ribs. The sauce is classic Thai, a combination of hot (jalapeño), sour (balsamic vinegar), salty (soy sauce and fish sauce), and sweet (honey).

3 to 4	pounds beef short ribs, preferably English cut (see headnote)
1	teaspoon kosher salt
½	teaspoon coarsely ground black pepper
	Nonstick oil spray
4	cloves garlic, minced
2	tablespoons minced gingerroot
3	tablespoons hoisin sauce
2	tablespoons balsamic vinegar

1½	tablespoons Thai or Vietnamese fish sauce (*nam pla* or *nuoc mam*)
1	tablespoon honey
1	tablespoon soy sauce
	Juice and finely grated zest of 1 lime
1	jalapeño pepper, stemmed, seeded, and finely chopped
3	scallions, cut into thin slices
2	tablespoons finely chopped fresh cilantro

PREHEAT a broiler on high. Season the meaty parts of the short ribs with salt and pepper and set bone-side down on a broiler tray. Spray with oil and broil until the meaty parts are browned, about 10 minutes. Transfer to a 5- to 6-quart slow cooker.

MIX together the garlic, ginger, hoisin sauce, vinegar, fish sauce, honey, soy sauce, and lime juice and zest in a small bowl, and pour over the short ribs. Cover the cooker and cook until the ribs are tender, 3 to 4 hours on high, or 6 to 8 hours on low.

TRANSFER the short ribs to a platter (you can remove the bones and discard, if you like). Skim the fat from the liquid and discard. Add the jalapeño, scallions, and cilantro and cook on high for 5 minutes. Spoon the sauce over the meat and serve.

SERVINGS

PRECOOK

10 minutes

SLOW COOK

3 to 4 hours on high, or 6 to 8 hours on low, in a 5- to 6-quart slow cooker

AT THE END

5 minutes

Jerk Pork and Yams

The fiery spice blend of Jamaica, known as jerk, radiates as much aroma as heat. Although macho jerk jerks may crave the fiery challenge, it's the characteristic fragrance of allspice and thyme that you want to capture in this hearty one-pot meal. Pork ribs (use country-style for more meat, less bone) are layered with sweet potatoes, jerk seasoning, and brown sugar. In the crucible of the slow cooker, the flavors meld together and the ribs become glazed with a sweet and spicy syrup.

6

SERVINGS

PRECOOK

10 minutes

SLOW COOK

3 to 4 hours on high, or 6 to 8 hours on low, in a 5- to 6-quart slow cooker

AT THE END

5 minutes

4	cloves garlic, minced
1	Scotch Bonnet or habanero pepper, stemmed, seeded, and finely chopped
1	teaspoon dried thyme
2	teaspoons ground allspice
3	tablespoons dark brown sugar
2	tablespoons dark rum
2	tablespoons vegetable oil
2	teaspoons kosher salt, divided
½	teaspoon coarsely ground black pepper, divided
3	pounds country-style pork ribs
2	tablespoons butter
2	pounds sweet potatoes, peeled and cut into ½-inch-thick slices
6	scallions, roots trimmed, cut into thin slices
1	large tomato, finely chopped

PREHEAT a broiler on medium-high or high. Mix together the garlic, hot pepper, thyme, allspice, brown sugar, rum, oil, and half the salt and pepper in a small bowl, and rub all over the ribs. Place the ribs on a broiler tray and brown on the broadest sides of the ribs, about 5 minutes per side.

DOT the bottom of the crock of a 5- to 6-quart slow cooker with butter and layer the sweet potatoes evenly in the cooker; season with the remaining salt and pepper. Arrange the ribs on top of the potatoes. Cover the cooker and cook until the ribs and potatoes are fork-tender, 3 to 4 hours on high, or 6 to 8 hours on low.

LIFT the potatoes and ribs from the cooker with a slotted spoon and arrange on a platter. Skim the fat from the juices in the cooker; stir the scallions and tomatoes into the juices in the cooker and spoon over the ribs. Serve immediately.

what else?

- Scotch Bonnet and habanero peppers are very hot and can be irritating to your skin, so wear rubber gloves when chopping them.

Espresso Braised Beef

When espresso beans—which are roasted until they are on the verge of burning—are teamed with beef, they yield a flavor complexity that has more kinship with the grill than with a cup of coffee. That's because our palates perceive things that are darkly roasted similarly, which explains why espresso has the surprising effect of making beef taste meatier. Here, this effect is enhanced by two other dark, savory ingredients: molasses and Worcestershire sauce. The result is a braised brisket that tastes like it spent hours being basted in a barbecue pit instead of cozily simmering in your slow cooker.

6-8

SERVINGS

PRECOOK

20 minutes plus
1 hour resting

SLOW COOK

4 to 6 hours on high,
or 8 to 10 hours on
low, in a 5- to 6-quart
slow cooker

AT THE END

10 minutes

2	tablespoons finely ground espresso coffee beans
1	tablespoon sugar
1	teaspoon garlic powder
½	teaspoon ground coriander
¼	teaspoon ground cumin, preferably ground from whole seeds toasted in a dry skillet
½	teaspoon coarsely ground black pepper
1	tablespoon kosher salt
2	tablespoons olive oil, divided

3	pounds beef brisket, trimmed of excess fat
1	large onion, chopped
1½	cups strong brewed coffee
2	tablespoons balsamic vinegar
¼	cup dark molasses
1	tablespoon Worcestershire sauce
2	whole cloves
3	tablespoons orange marmalade

MIX the ground coffee, sugar, garlic powder, coriander, cumin, black pepper, and salt together in a small bowl. Rub all over the brisket, wrap in plastic wrap, and let rest for 1 hour.

HEAT 1 tablespoon of the oil in a large skillet over medium-high heat. Brown the brisket on both sides, about 5 minutes per side, starting fatty-side down. Transfer to a 5- to 6-quart slow cooker.

ADD the remaining tablespoon of oil to the skillet. Add the onion and cook until browned, about 3 minutes. Add the brewed coffee, vinegar, molasses, and Worcestershire sauce and bring to a boil. Pour over the brisket and throw the cloves into the liquid. Cover the cooker and cook on high for 4 to 6 hours, or on low for 8 to 10 hours, until the meat is fork-tender.

TRANSFER the brisket to a cutting board. Skim the fat from the surface of the juices in the cooker, and remove and discard the cloves. While the brisket rests, heat the juices on high for 10 minutes, and stir in the marmalade. Slice the brisket across its grain and arrange the slices so they overlap on a large platter. Ladle enough sauce over the top to moisten, and serve with the remaining sauce on the side.

what else?

- Feel free to use different cuts of beef. The dark-roasted succulence of this brisket is equally good on short ribs or beef chuck, for example. They will all cook in the same amount of time.

- Like most braised meats, brisket is better the second day. Slice it and hold it in its gravy in the refrigerator, and then heat it in the cooker on high for about an hour.

Salmon Slow-Cooked with Herbs

Salmon is one of the few fish sturdy enough for braising, but like all fish, it can be ruined by over-cooking. So for this recipe, you will need either a cooker with a timer that allows it to switch to warm automatically, or you will have to reserve this dish for a day when you will be around to monitor the cooking. The setup of the cooker is also a bit unusual: a layer of vegetables is topped with a strip of foil, onto which you place the salmon. This construction has a double benefit: The foil barrier causes the vegetables to cook faster than the fish, so they are both done at the same time. It also acts as a sling for lifting the fish without damaging it. Vegetables and salmon are glazed elegantly with a buttery herb sauce made from the reduced cooking liquid.

2   tablespoons extra-virgin olive oil, divided

1   pound small Yukon Gold potatoes, scrubbed and cut into thin slices

1   medium onion, halved and cut into thin slices

2   celery ribs, cut into thin slices

2   pounds farm-raised salmon fillet, pin bones removed

½   teaspoon kosher salt, plus more to taste

¼   teaspoon coarsely ground black pepper, plus more to taste

½   cup dry white wine

1   cup hot water

2   tablespoons chopped fresh herbs, such as parsley, dill, basil, and/or tarragon

2   tablespoons butter

DRIZZLE the bottom of a 5- to 6-quart oval slow cooker with 1 tablespoon of the olive oil. Layer the potatoes, onion, and celery over the bottom. Place a 2-foot length of 12-inch-wide heavy-duty aluminum foil lengthwise across the cooker and press down so that it covers the vegetables and the sides of the crock, and the ends of the foil extend over the rim at each end of the crock.

SEASON the flesh side of the salmon with ½ teaspoon salt and ¼ teaspoon pepper. Heat the remaining 1 tablespoon olive oil in a large heavy skillet over high heat. Brown the flesh side of the salmon in the oil, about 2 minutes. Place the salmon, skin side down, on top of the foil.

CONTINUED

SERVINGS

PRECOOK

10 minutes

SLOW COOK

2½ to 3 hours on low in a 5- to 6-quart oval slow cooker

AT THE END

10 minutes

Salmon Slow-Cooked with Herbs CONTINUED

ADD the wine to the pan and heat to boiling. Stir in the water and pour over the salmon. Set the skillet aside for later use. Cover the cooker and cook on low for 2½ to 3 hours, until the salmon flakes when pressed gently. You can keep the salmon on warm for several hours.

TO SERVE, use the foil to lift the salmon from the cooker and transfer to a large platter. Lift the vegetables from the cooker with a slotted spoon and arrange around the fish. Pour the liquid from the cooker into the skillet and bring to a boil over high heat. Boil until reduced to about ¾ cup of liquid. Add the herbs and boil for 1 minute; remove from the heat and swirl in the butter. Adjust the seasoning with more salt and pepper and pour the sauce over the fish and vegetables. Serve immediately.

what else?

- It is important to use farm-raised, rather than wild, salmon in a slow cooker. Wild fish do not develop as much fat as their more sedentary farm-raised cousins, and they tend to dry during cooking. They are fine for grilling or baking, but are not an option for the slow cooker.

- For a change, try thin slices of carrot and bell pepper in place of the potatoes and celery.

Pork Sirloin Braised with White Beans, Rosemary, and Sage

This Italian-inspired pork-and-beans dish smells of garlic, rosemary, and sage. It swells with wine and a blush of tomato, and travels as far away from the sweet, smoky, ketchup-laden American version as a dish can go without being expatriated. The herbal assault happens on three fronts: first as a dry rub, then when half of a fresh herb mixture is cooked with the pork, and finally when the rest is swirled into the sauce at the end for a final olfactory onslaught.

1	teaspoon dried sage
1	teaspoon dried rosemary, crushed
3	large cloves garlic, 1 minced and 2 halved
1	teaspoon kosher salt
½	teaspoon ground black pepper
4	tablespoons extra-virgin olive oil
2½	pounds boneless pork sirloin, rolled and tied
1	onion, diced
1	cup dry white wine

1	can (about 15 ounces) fire-roasted diced tomatoes, drained
2	cans (about 15 ounces) cannellini beans, drained and rinsed
¼	cup coarsely chopped fresh sage
1	teaspoon chopped fresh rosemary
¼	cup coarsely chopped fresh Italian (flat-leaf) parsley
2	tablespoons toasted pine nuts (see page 73)

SERVINGS

PRECOOK

30 minutes

SLOW COOK

6 hours on low in a 5- to 6-quart slow cooker

AT THE END

5 minutes

MIX the dried sage, rosemary, minced garlic, salt, and pepper in a small bowl, and rub all over the pork. Heat the olive oil in a large skillet over medium-high heat and brown the pork on all sides, about 4 minutes per side. Transfer the pork to a 5- to 6-quart slow cooker.

ADD the onion to the oil remaining in the skillet, reduce the heat to medium, and sauté until browned, about 5 minutes. Add the wine and boil until mostly evaporated. Add the tomatoes and beans and heat to boiling; set aside.

PROCESS the fresh sage, rosemary, parsley, and garlic clove halves in a minichopper or small food processor until finely chopped. Add the oil and pine nuts and process or chop for a second, just until combined. Stir half of the herb mixture into the tomato-bean mixture, and pour over the pork. Set the remaining herb mixture aside. Cover the cooker and cook on low for 6 hours, until the pork is fork-tender.

CONTINUED

Pork Sirloin Braised with
White Beans, Rosemary, and Sage CONTINUED

REMOVE the pork to a cutting board to rest. Turn the cooker to high and bring the liquid to a boil. Stir in the remaining herb mixture, and remove the beans to a serving platter with a slotted spoon. Snip the string or net from the pork, slice, and arrange around the beans on the platter so the slices overlap. Spoon the cooking liquid over the pork and serve.

what else?

- Although cannellini beans are the most traditional bean to cook with pork, you can use any white bean, such as navy beans, pea beans, butter beans, or Great Northern beans.

- Pork sirloin is a little leaner than shoulder. It's fine to use pork shoulder in this preparation, but you will want to cook it a bit longer, about 8 hours.

Braised Turkey Thighs with Posole and Lime

Posole is Mexican hominy. It is sold dried or canned. Both are easy to cook, but dried posole requires soaking. Even after many hours in the slow cooker, dried posole has a tendency to remain unpleasantly crunchy, so I use canned exclusively. Posole has a unique astringency that is enhanced by lime and cilantro; the three are such a common triumvirate that dishes containing all three are often known by the name of the grain. The most famous of these is turkey posole, a brothy soup that is the inspiration for this stew. Turkey thighs are extremely forgiving when braised in a slow cooker. Although it is almost impossible to overcook them, they also reach doneness much earlier than you might expect. You can use this to your advantage by speeding up the cooking on high (the thighs will be done in about 3 hours), or letting them simmer languorously all day.

¼   cup flour

1   teaspoon kosher salt

¼   teaspoon coarsely ground black pepper

3   pounds turkey thighs, skin removed

2   tablespoon extra-virgin olive oil

¾   cup mild salsa

1   cup chicken broth

1   can (about 16 ounces) white posole, drained and rinsed

Juice and finely grated zest of 1 large lime

2   tablespoons chopped fresh cilantro

MIX the flour, salt, and pepper in a medium mixing bowl. Add the turkey thighs and turn to coat with seasoned flour; pat off the excess flour and reserve the seasoned flour mixture.

HEAT the oil in a large heavy skillet over medium-high heat. Brown the turkey on both sides, about 4 minutes per side, and place in a 5- to 6-quart slow cooker.

ADD the reserved seasoned flour to the oil left in the skillet, and cook for 30 seconds, stirring constantly. Add the salsa and broth to the skillet and bring to a boil, stirring until slightly thickened. Stir in the posole and lime zest (but not the juice). Pour over the turkey.

COVER the cooker and cook for 3 to 4 hours on high, or 5 to 8 hours on low, until the turkey registers at least 170°F on an instant-read thermometer. Stir in the lime juice and serve.

4

SERVINGS

PRECOOK

15 minutes

SLOW COOK

3 to 4 hours on high, or 5 to 8 hours on low, in a 5- to 6-quart slow cooker

Lamb Shanks Braised with Prunes and Brandy

Pity the prune. Bloated and wrinkly as a dishwasher's hands, and better known as a digestive than as a food to savor, the prune appears more often as the butt of a joke than an ingredient in a recipe. What a shame, for the fruitiness of prune is all-purpose, moving elegantly from compote to stew and lending its deep, dark sweetness without seeking credit or attention in return. In this recipe it blends elegantly with the slight gaminess of lamb, taming its rough edges and underscoring its velvety richness. The sauce is finished with either prune butter or lekvar, a Hungarian prune pastry filling. You should be able to find either one in the baking section of your market. If you can't, you can make some lekvar by mashing a finely chopped pitted prune with 2 tablespoons boiling water.

1	tablespoon curry powder or garam masala	3	tablespoons extra-virgin olive oil, divided
1	teaspoon ground cumin, preferably ground from whole seeds toasted in a dry skillet	2	large onions, coarsely shredded
1	teaspoon ground aniseed	2	cloves garlic, minced
2	teaspoons kosher salt	2	tablespoons flour
4	lamb shanks (about 1 pound each)	½	cup full-bodied red wine, such as Shiraz
½	cup brandy	1	cup beef broth
12	large pitted prunes	2	tablespoons prune butter or lekvar

MIX the curry powder, cumin, aniseed, and salt together in a small bowl, and rub half of the mixture over the lamb shanks. Let rest for 20 to 30 minutes. Set aside the remaining spice mixture.

MEANWHILE, heat the brandy in a deep saucepan over medium heat until steaming. Add the prunes, toss to coat, cover, and set aside for 30 minutes.

HEAT half the olive oil in a large heavy skillet over medium-high heat; brown the lamb shanks on all sides and place in a single layer in a 5- to 6-quart slow cooker.

CONTINUED

SERVINGS

PRECOOK
25 minutes
plus 30 minutes resting

SLOW COOK
4 to 5 hours on high,
or 6 to 8 hours on
low, in a 5- to 6-quart
slow cooker

Lamb Shanks Braised with Prunes and Brandy CONTINUED

ADD the remaining olive oil to the skillet, reduce the heat to medium, add the onions, and sauté until lightly browned, about 5 minutes, stirring often. Add the garlic and flour and continue cooking until everything is well browned, about 3 more minutes, stirring constantly. Add the wine and bring to a boil, stirring constantly. Stir in the broth and the reserved spice mix. Heat to boiling, stirring until slightly thickened. Pour over the shanks and add the brandy and prunes. Cover the cooker and cook until the lamb is fork-tender, 4 to 5 hours on high, or 6 to 8 hours on low.

TRANSFER the shanks to a serving platter with tongs. Skim the fat from the liquid remaining in the cooker and stir in the prune butter. Spoon the sauce and prunes over the lamb shanks, and serve.

what else?

- This recipe may also be made with a 4-pound lamb shoulder roast or 2 pounds of lamb cubes.

- It is fine to make this recipe ahead and refrigerate it for a day or two, but if you do, you will find that much of the liquid has been absorbed by the prunes. This can be remedied by adding ¼ to ½ cup water when reheating.

Boneless Pork Ribs Braised with Fennel and Olives

Meaty and thick, boneless country-style pork ribs don't lend themselves to finger licking and bone sucking, but they slow-cook beautifully. Fragrant with fennel and olives, in the style of French Mediterranean cuisine, this dish enhances the most elegant dinner. I would serve it with risotto or roasted potatoes, but it would also be good with garlic-scented pasta (spinach pasta would be beautiful with the fennel). Or just serve a warm loaf of crusty bread.

SERVINGS

PRECOOK

20 minutes

SLOW COOK

3 to 4 hours on high, or 6 to 8 hours on low, in a 5- to 6-quart slow cooker

AT THE END

5 minutes

¼	cup flour
2	teaspoons ground fennel seed
1	teaspoon kosher salt
¼	teaspoon coarsely ground black pepper
2	pounds boneless country-style pork ribs
⅓	cup extra-virgin olive oil, divided
1	large fennel bulb, stems and leaves trimmed, cut lengthwise into ½-inch-thick slices
1	medium onion, cut into ½-inch dice

8	cloves garlic, minced
1	teaspoon chopped fresh rosemary
½	cup dry white wine
1	cup chicken broth
1	cup canned diced tomatoes, drained
½	cup halved pitted black olives, preferably kalamata
2	tablespoons coarsely chopped fresh Italian (flat-leaf) parsley

MIX the flour, fennel seed, salt, and pepper in a medium mixing bowl. Coat the meat in the seasoned flour mixture; pat off the excess flour and reserve the mixture.

HEAT half the olive oil in a large deep skillet (preferably cast-iron) over medium-high heat. Add the pork and brown lightly on both sides, about 3 minutes per side. Transfer to a plate and set aside.

ADD the rest of the oil to the skillet. Dredge the fennel slices in some of the reserved seasoned flour and brown on both sides, about 2 minutes per side. Arrange over the bottom of a 5- to 6-quart slow cooker, and place the pork on top.

ADD the onion to the skillet and cook over medium heat until tender, but not browned, about 3 minutes. Add the garlic and rosemary and stir once or twice. Stir in the remaining seasoned flour and continue stirring until the onions are uniformly coated. Stir in the wine and bring to a boil. Add the broth and tomatoes and stir until slightly thickened. Pour into the slow cooker. Cover the cooker and cook 3 to 4 hours on high, or 6 to 8 hours on low, until the pork is fork-tender.

SCATTER the olives and parsley over the meat, cover, and cook for 5 minutes more. Serve immediately.

what else?

- Fennel is also called anise. Whatever you call it, buy fennel with a large heavy bulb and as few dark green stalks as possible. The stalks are very fibrous and the leaves are not flavorful, so they should be trimmed before cooking.

Oxtails Braised in Fragrant Coconut Milk

Oxtails, one of the few foods that wag, meet their righteous end in the confines of a slow cooker. The meat, which is tough and stringy at best, softens to plush as it simmers. The abundance of cartilage melts, lending body to the broth, while the traces of fat that are threaded through meat infuse the developing sauce with a rich, meaty flavor. Add to this a flare of curry and a balm of coconut milk, and you have a braised dish like no other. If you can't find oxtails in your local food store, look again; they might be in the freezer. If that doesn't work, you can substitute beef or veal shanks.

SERVINGS

PRECOOK
20 minutes

SLOW COOK
4 to 5 hours on high, or 8 to 10 hours on low, in a 5- to 6-quart slow cooker

AT THE END
5 minutes

¼	cup flour
1	teaspoon kosher salt
¼	teaspoon coarsely ground black pepper
1	tablespoon ground coriander
1	teaspoon ground cumin, preferably ground from whole seeds toasted in a dry skillet
⅛	teaspoon ground allspice
6	large pieces oxtail (about 12 ounces each)
½	teaspoon ground turmeric
2	tablespoons vegetable oil
1	medium onion, chopped

2	carrots, peeled and finely diced
3	cloves garlic, minced
1	tablespoon finely chopped gingerroot
1	cup beef broth
¾	cup fat-free coconut milk
1	cup canned diced tomato, drained
1	cinnamon stick
6	cardamom pods
2	bay leaves
2	tablespoons chopped fresh cilantro

MIX the flour, salt, pepper, coriander, cumin, and allspice in a medium-large mixing bowl. Roll the oxtails in the spiced flour mixture until they are coated on all sides. Remove and pat off excess spiced flour. Add the turmeric to the remaining flour mixture and set aside.

HEAT the oil in a large deep skillet, preferably cast-iron, over medium-high heat. Brown the oxtails on all sides, about 4 minutes per side, in batches if necessary; do not crowd the pan. Transfer to a 5- to 6-quart slow cooker.

ADD the onion and carrots to the skillet and sauté over medium heat until tender and browned, about 4 minutes. Add the garlic and ginger and cook for 30 seconds, stirring often. Add the reserved spiced flour mixture and stir to coat the vegetables. Stir in the broth, coconut milk, and tomato, and boil, stirring often, until the sauce is slightly thickened.

TUCK the cinnamon stick, cardamom pods, and bay leaves around the pieces of oxtail, and pour the sauce over all. Cover the cooker and cook for 4 to 5 hours on high, or 8 to 10 hours on low, until the oxtails are very tender.

TRANSFER the oxtails to a platter, skim the fat from the sauce in the cooker, remove the bay leaves and cinnamon stick, and stir in the cilantro. Pour the sauce over the oxtails and serve.

Slow-Cooked Classics

IN THE INBRED WORLD OF FOOD SNOBS, gourmands have been known to come to blows over whether a bouillabaisse is a bouillabaisse without rascasse, the bony fish of the Mediterranean that's more skeleton than meat. There are heated debates over the origins of pasta, and near-brawls to determine whether the most authentic version of cassoulet is from Castelnaudary, Carcassonne, or Toulouse. The trouble with these discussions is not that they lack interest, but simply that they aren't useful.

Cooking is at heart a folk art, and we do it a disservice whenever we take its products too seriously. For the quality of any dish does not lie in the purity of its recipe or the authenticity of its ingredients, but in the way that it fits the taste, lifestyle, and dining habits of those who choose to cook it and eat it.

Don't get me wrong. I am not a proponent of canned cassoulet, but I do advocate fiddling with classic recipes, or any recipes for that matter, that seem overly complex, expensive, or time-consuming.

It is this embrace of creative shortcuts that has led me to this chapter—a celebration of classic dishes reinvented for the slow cooker. It is a wonder that many of them, including Barbecued Beef (page 122), Bollito Misto (page 138), Beef Carbonnade (page 144), and All-Day Cassoulet (page 135), ever developed before the advent of the slow cooker. That is, until you realize that in the premodern kitchen, if you weren't roasting over an open flame, you were slow-cooking in some form, either on the back of a wood-burning stove, in the embers of a dying fire, or in the latent warmth of a stone-lined hearth.

CHAPTER 4

Recipes

Barbecued Beef

What's barbecue without fire? Convenient. I know there's no flavor of wood smoke, but there's also no tending a fire for 8 hours. Contrary to popular opinion, the only essential element for successful barbecue is long slow heat and sufficient moisture to relax the fibers of tough meat into submission. That makes barbecue a natural for the slow cooker, with all the expected melt-in-your-mouth results, while you're off riding on the range. Feel free to alter the flavor by varying the spice rub or sauce.

6

SERVINGS

PRECOOK

15 minutes

SLOW COOK

6 to 10 hours on low
in a 5- to 6-quart
slow cooker

AT THE END

10 minutes

3	**pounds beef chuck pot roast**
2	**tablespoons Southwest-style spice rub, homemade (page 68) or purchased**

1	**tablespoon vegetable oil**
1	**cup barbecue sauce, homemade (page 69) or purchased**

SEASON the beef with the spice rub. Heat the oil in a large skillet over high heat. Brown the beef on both sides in the hot oil, about 5 minutes per side; it's fine if it scorches a bit on the edges. Transfer to a 5- to 6-quart slow cooker.

POUR the barbecue sauce over the beef and turn to coat. Cover the cooker and cook on low for 6 to 10 hours, or until the beef is easily pierced with a fork.

REMOVE the beef to a cutting board and rest for 10 minutes. Skim the fat off the juices. Slice the beef across the grain and serve with the juices.

Corned Beef, Potatoes, and Sauerkraut

Corned beef and cabbage is a classic candidate for a sojourn in a slow cooker. Here the cabbage is replaced with sauerkraut, which makes all the difference. And since corned beef brisket is cured, it doesn't need to be browned, which makes it well suited for slow cooking. This recipe couldn't be easier; just layer everything in the cooker and plug it in.

1	corned beef brisket (about 2½ pounds)
2	medium onions, quartered
1	bag (about 32 ounces) refrigerated sauerkraut, drained and rinsed
2	pounds small round potatoes, red-skin or golden, halved

	Ground black pepper
¼	teaspoon ground allspice
1	can (about 12 ounces) beer
1	bay leaf
	Spicy brown mustard or horseradish (optional)

PLACE the corned beef, fat side down, in a 5- to 6-quart slow cooker. Add the onions, sauerkraut, and potatoes in even layers. Season with pepper to taste and allspice, pour the beer over all, and nestle a bay leaf in the center. Cover the cooker and cook for 4 to 5 hours on high, or 8 to 10 hours on low, until the corned beef and potatoes are tender. Discard the bay leaf and onion quarters.

LIFT the potatoes with tongs or a slotted spoon and arrange around the perimeter of the serving platter. Mound the sauerkraut in the center. Carefully transfer the corned beef to a cutting board and cut across the grain into thick slices. Arrange on top of the sauerkraut, and spoon some of the cooking liquid over the meat. Serve with spicy brown mustard or horseradish, if desired.

6-8

SERVINGS

PRECOOK
5 minutes

SLOW COOK
4 to 5 hours on high, or 8 to 10 hours on low, in a 5- to 6-quart slow cooker

Slow-Cooked Chicken Dinner

If a pot of savory stew could be a vehicle for time travel, this one would transport us to a long-gone country kitchen, where an iron pot of simmering vegetables, broth, and herbs was transforming a chicken into dinner. Back then the stove was stoked with wood or coal, the fire was constant and low, and boiled dinners like this were daily fare. Although dishes like this one have fallen out of fashion, few recipes transform a kitchen into the heart of a home more magically than it can. Be sure to use a large chicken. The parts will cook more slowly and be more succulent than those of a smaller chicken.

⅓	cup flour
¼	cup All-Purpose Spice Rub (page 127)
1	roasting chicken (about 7 pounds)
1½	pounds medium golden or red-skin potatoes, quartered
2	tablespoons vegetable oil, divided
1	large onion, cut into chunks

24	baby-cut carrots
4	celery ribs, cut into ¾-inch lengths
½	cup dry white wine
2	cups chicken broth
3	tablespoons instant mashed potato flakes
2	tablespoons chopped fresh Italian (flat-leaf) parsley

MIX the flour and spice rub in a medium mixing bowl. Cut the chicken into 6 pieces: 2 drumsticks, 2 thighs, and 2 breast halves with wings attached and the pointed joints of the wings removed. Take off the skin from all pieces except the wings. Turn the chicken pieces in the flour mixture until thoroughly coated; pat off the excess flour and reserve the flour mixture.

BOIL the potatoes in several quarts of lightly salted water for 5 minutes; drain and place in the bottom of a 5- to 6-quart slow cooker.

HEAT half the oil in a large heavy skillet over medium-high heat. Brown the chicken on both sides, about 4 minutes per side, and transfer to a plate; set aside.

CONTINUED

6-8

SERVINGS

PRECOOK
20 minutes

SLOW COOK
3 to 4 hours on high,
or 5 to 6 hours on
low, in a 5- to 6-quart
slow cooker

AT THE END
3 to 4 minutes

Slow-Cooked Chicken Dinner CONTINUED

ADD the remaining oil to the skillet. Add the onion, carrots, and celery and sauté until lightly browned, about 5 minutes. Add the reserved seasoned flour and stir until the vegetables are coated. Add the wine and bring to a boil. Add the chicken broth and simmer until slightly thickened; pour into the cooker. Arrange the drumsticks and thighs on top of the vegetables and the breast halves on top of the dark meat. Cover the cooker and cook for 3 to 4 hours on high, or 5 to 6 hours on low, until an instant-read thermometer inserted into the thickest part of one of the breast pieces registers 165°F.

REMOVE the chicken to a serving platter and surround with the potatoes, carrots, and celery; keep warm. Turn the cooker up to high, stir in the instant mashed potato flakes, and continue stirring until the gravy thickens slightly, about 3 minutes. Stir in the parsley and spoon over the chicken.

all-purpose spice rub

Makes ¼ cup

1   tablespoon light brown sugar

1   tablespoon kosher salt

1   teaspoon paprika

1   teaspoon dry mustard

1   teaspoon ground dried sage

1   teaspoon dried thyme

½   teaspoon dried rosemary, crushed

½   teaspoon garlic powder

½   teaspoon coarsely ground
    black pepper

MIX all ingredients together in a small bowl.

Baked Rigatoni

The temperature in a slow cooker is ideal for baked casseroles. Flavors merge and mingle, the sauce has time to permeate every nook in every noodle, and a crunchy crust forms at the edge, protecting the interior from too much heat. The crust can burn, just as it does in the oven, so the timing is tighter for slow-cooked casseroles than it is for moist preparations like stews and soups. You cannot leave for the day unless you have a cooker that will switch to warm automatically. Most casseroles, including this classic baked rigatoni, can rest at warm for several hours without harm.

12 ounces rigatoni pasta

2½ tablespoons extra-virgin olive oil

1 onion, finely chopped

1 celery rib, finely diced

1 red or green bell pepper, seeded, deribbed, and finely diced

1 jar (about 26 ounces) chunky marinara sauce

1 can (about 10¾ ounces) condensed cream of mushroom soup

½ teaspoon salt

¼ teaspoon ground black pepper

8 ounces mozzarella cheese, shredded

¼ cup shredded Parmesan cheese

BRING a large pot of lightly salted water to a boil. Add the rigatoni, stir once to moisten, and boil until barely tender, about 8 minutes.

MEANWHILE, heat 2 tablespoons of the oil in a large deep skillet over medium heat. Add the onion, celery, and bell pepper and sauté until tender, about 4 minutes. Add the marinara sauce, mushroom soup, salt, and pepper and bring to a boil, stirring often. Remove from the heat. Drain the cooked pasta thoroughly and stir into the sauce.

COAT the interior of a 5- to 6-quart slow cooker with the remaining ½ tablespoon of oil. Put a third of the pasta on the bottom of the cooker and cover with half the mozzarella. Repeat the layers and put the remaining pasta on top. Cover the cooker and cook for 2 to 3 hours on high, or 4 to 6 hours on low.

SPRINKLE the top with the Parmesan, cover, and cook on high for about 10 minutes, or until the cheese melts. Keep warm for up to 1 hour or serve immediately.

4-6

SERVINGS

PRECOOK

20 minutes

SLOW COOK

2 to 3 hours on high, or 4 to 6 hours on low, in a 5- to 6-quart slow cooker

AT THE END

10 minutes

My Mother's Meat Loaf

My mother, though a hopeless cook, was a meat-loaf savant. She willed me her recipe, and though I didn't think it could be improved, moving it into a slow cooker has made its velvety texture even smoother. Delicious on the first night, it is even better the next day for sandwiches.

4-6

SERVINGS

PRECOOK

10 minutes

SLOW COOK

3 to 4 hours on high, or 6 to 7 hours on low, in a 5- to 6-quart slow cooker

2   slices bread, preferably rye, crusts removed, and crumbled

½   cup milk

1   medium onion, coarsely grated

2   large eggs

½   cup ketchup

1   tablespoon Worcestershire sauce

2   teaspoons spicy brown mustard

½   teaspoon salt

¼   teaspoon ground black pepper

2   pounds meat loaf blend (50% beef, 25% veal, 25% pork)

Ketchup (optional)

PLACE a 2-foot length of 12-inch-wide, heavy-duty aluminum foil across the length of a 5- to 6-quart oval slow cooker. Press the foil against the bottom and sides, leaving the ends of the foil extending over the rim at each end of the cooker.

COMBINE the bread and milk in a large mixing bowl and squeeze with your hands until the bread is moist and mushy. Add the onion, eggs, ketchup, Worcestershire sauce, mustard, salt, and pepper and mix until fully blended. Add the meat and mix with your hands until the mixture is as smooth as possible. Scrape onto the foil in the slow cooker and form into an oval-shaped loaf. Cover the cooker and cook for 3 to 4 hours on high, or 6 to 7 hours on low, until an instant-read thermometer inserted in the center of the meat registers at least 160°F.

USE the foil to lift the meat loaf from the cooker, allowing any juices to remain behind, and transfer to a cutting board. Scrape away any coagulated drippings that may be clinging to the outside of the meat loaf and discard. Slice and serve with ketchup, if desired.

what else?

- Leftover meat loaf can be kept, tightly wrapped, in the refrigerator for 3 to 4 days. Warm the slices in a low oven or serve them cold like a pâté with a selection of mustards and pickles.

Mahogany Chicken Legs

The windows of Chinese delicatessens are crowded with glistening mahogany chickens, which look like they have been roasted in a hot oven but were actually slowly braised in soy sauce and spices. This ancient technique, known as red cooking, is mostly used with chicken and pork. The result is exceptionally moist meat that is falling-off-the-bone tender and saturated with flavor. Fortunately, red cooking is also a natural for a slow cooker. Red cooking depends on two types of soy sauce—the regular thin salty soy sauce you are used to and a thick, less salty soy, called dark (or black) soy sauce. The dark soy is essential; you cannot red-cook with regular soy sauce alone.

2	tablespoons vegetable oil	¼	cup dark brown sugar
6	whole large chicken legs, preferably from roasting chickens (about 6 pounds)	1	teaspoon Szechuan peppercorns or black peppercorns
1	cup dark soy sauce	2	slices gingerroot, peeled
1	cup light soy sauce	2	whole star anise, or 2 teaspoons aniseed
½	cup dry sherry or Shaoxing wine	1	teaspoon toasted sesame oil
3	tablespoons Chinkiang vinegar or balsamic vinegar	2	scallions, trimmed and cut into thin slices

HEAT the vegetable oil in a large heavy skillet over medium heat. Add the chicken and cook in batches until the skin dries on the surface but doesn't brown, about 2 minutes per side. Arrange, skin side down, in an even layer in a 5- to 6-quart slow cooker.

ADD the soy sauces, sherry, vinegar, brown sugar, peppercorns, ginger, and star anise to the skillet and bring to a boil. Pour over the chicken, cover the cooker, and cook for 3 to 4 hours on high, or 5 to 7 hours on low.

TRANSFER the chicken to a serving platter, drizzle with sesame oil, and scatter scallions over the top. Serve immediately.

6

SERVINGS

PRECOOK

10 minutes

SLOW COOK

3 to 4 hours on high, or 5 to 7 hours on low, in a 5- to 6-quart slow cooker

CONTINUED

Mahogany Chicken Legs CONTINUED

what else?

- Mahogany Chicken Legs can be served with hot boiled rice or Asian noodles, but it is also good taken off the bone and used to flavor a stir-fry or an Asian noodle salad.

- Light soy sauce is the most commonly available type of soy sauce. (It is not the same thing as "lite" or reduced-sodium soy sauce.) Dark soy sauce (a.k.a. black soy sauce) is aged longer, and is richer, thicker, and less salty. You might find it in a well-stocked Asian section of a supermarket, but you will probably have to go to a Chinese grocery store. Do not use thick soy sauce, which is molasses punched up with fermented soy extract.

- Shaoxing wine is a fermented rice wine that has the mellow character of dry sherry. Chinkiang vinegar, or black rice vinegar, is made by fermenting glutinous sweet rice. A good quality Chinkiang vinegar is made from just rice, water, and salt and is very similar in flavor to Italian balsamic vinegar. Check the ingredients, and avoid Chinkiang vinegars that contain sugar and caramel coloring, which can throw the subtle sweet and sour balance off. Shaoxing wine and Chinkiang vinegar are available in most Chinese grocery stores.

Barbecued Pork Ribs

The tenderness and succulence of barbecue in a slow cooker is unsurpassed, moister than barbecue from an open fire, and just as flavorful as meat that has been slow-cooked on a gas grill. These easy barbecued pork ribs prove my point with their juiciness, tenderness, and deep, rich barbecue tang. Although you could use any type of pork rib in this recipe, you will get meatier results with country-style ribs. They are cut from the shoulder end of the loin, making them similar in flavor and succulence to barbecued pork shoulder.

3	pounds country-style pork ribs		3	tablespoons honey
1	teaspoon kosher salt		3	tablespoons light brown sugar
¼	teaspoon coarsely ground black pepper		3	tablespoons apple cider vinegar
	Nonstick oil spray		1	teaspoon mild hot pepper sauce, such as Frank's Red Hot
¾	cup ketchup			
3	tablespoons spicy brown mustard			

PREHEAT a broiler on high. Season the ribs with the salt and pepper, set on a broiler tray, and spray with oil. Broil until the meaty parts are browned on both sides, 4 to 5 minutes per side. Transfer to a 5- to 6-quart slow cooker.

MIX the ketchup, mustard, honey, brown sugar, vinegar, and hot sauce in a small bowl and pour over the ribs. Cover the cooker and cook until the ribs are tender, 3 to 4 hours on high, or 6 to 8 hours on low. Remove the ribs to a platter and serve.

6

SERVINGS

PRECOOK
10 minutes

SLOW COOK
3 to 4 hours on high, or 6 to 8 hours on low, in a 5- to 6-quart slow cooker

All-Day Cassoulet

Last year I made this traditional French country casserole for a Super Bowl party. As a result, my sons will always think of it not as the legendary Languedoc amalgam of beans and meats that has inspired endless recipes, but as the classic Super Bowl gut-buster. They're right. Cassoulet is peasant food, built to assuage hunger so completely that no amount of labor or hardship could dent the cloud of contentment it generates. And though foodies may argue about authenticity and the precise balance of meat to beans, and whether breadcrumbs belong on top, the truth is, a cassoulet is made from whatever you have on hand. Mine has white beans, lamb, garlic sausage, and smoked sausage (*and* breadcrumbs), but you can make yours with pork or ham, goat, or duck. Whatever you use, keep the proportions similar to those listed below, and you can't lose. Go Eagles!

1   pound dried large white beans, such as cannellini or baby limas

1   duck (about 4 pounds)

1   pound boneless leg of lamb, cut into 2-inch cubes

2   teaspoons kosher salt

½   teaspoon coarsely ground black pepper

8   ounces garlic sausage, cut into 2-inch lengths

8   ounces smoked sausage, such as andouille, cut into 2-inch lengths

1   large onion, diced

2   large celery ribs, cut into ¼-inch-thick slices

4   cloves garlic, minced

¼   teaspoon ground nutmeg

1   teaspoon dried Italian seasoning

    Pinch of ground cloves

½   cup dry white wine

4   cups beef or chicken broth, or a mixture

1   can (about 15 ounces) diced tomatoes, drained

⅔   cup dried breadcrumbs

¼   cup coarsely chopped fresh Italian (flat-leaf) parsley

12

SERVINGS

PRECOOK

1½ hours to overnight (depending on how you soak the beans)

SLOW COOK

8 to 10 hours on low in a 5- to 6-quart cooker

AT THE END

40 minutes

PUT the beans in a medium bowl, cover with about 3 inches of water, and soak overnight. Or put the beans in a saucepan, cover with water, and bring to a boil for 3 minutes. Remove from the heat and soak for 1 hour. Then drain.

MEANWHILE, cut the duck into 8 pieces: 2 breast halves, 2 drumsticks, 2 thighs, and 2 wings. Trim off all visible fat and excess skin and set the fat and skin aside. Season the duck pieces and lamb with the salt and pepper and set aside.

COOK the duck fat and skin in a large heavy skillet over medium heat until between ¼ and ⅓ cup fat is in the pan, about 4 minutes. Remove the solid pieces of fat and skin and discard. Brown the duck in the hot fat on both sides, about 4 minutes per side, and set aside. Brown the lamb, about 4 minutes per side, and set aside. Brown the sausage pieces on all sides, about 3 minutes per side, and set aside.

CONTINUED

All-Day Cassoulet CONTINUED

ADD the onion and celery to the skillet and sauté until lightly browned, about 4 minutes. Add the garlic, nutmeg, Italian seasoning, and cloves and sauté until aromatic, about 1 minute. Add the wine and bring to a boil. Add the beef broth and tomatoes, return to a boil, and remove from the heat.

TO ASSEMBLE THE CASSOULET, layer the beans and meats, in alternating layers (4 of beans, 3 of meat), starting and ending with the beans. Pour the liquid over all, cover the cooker, and cook until the beans are tender, 8 to 10 hours on low.

PREHEAT an oven to 350°F. Mix the breadcrumbs and parsley and scatter over the top of the cassoulet. Transfer the crock with the cassoulet to the oven and bake until the top is browned and bubbling, about 30 minutes. Serve immediately.

Bollito Misto

Boiled dinners, from pot au feu to corned beef and cabbage, exist in every cuisine with access to water and fire. *Bollito misto*, the Italian version (it translates as "mixed boil"), abounds with a variety of meat and vegetables. As the ingredients simmer, they create a beautiful broth, which is the genius of all boiled dinners. Though everything cooks in a single vessel, the meal that emerges is a multi-course one. Serve the broth as a soup in a bowl with baby pasta and diced tomato; the meat and vegetables, accompanied by a pesto mayonnaise, are the main course; and if you are feeling particularly continental, you can serve the marrow from the veal shanks separately, spread on warm toast.

6

SERVINGS

PRECOOK

10 minutes

SLOW COOK

6 to 8 hours on low, in a 6-quart, or larger, slow cooker

AT THE END

15 minutes

FOR THE BOLLITO MISTO

1	large onion, cut into 1-inch chunks
2	carrots, cut into 1-inch chunks
2	fennel ribs, cut into 1-inch-thick slices
2	turnips, peeled and cut into 1-inch chunks
	Salt
	Ground black pepper
3	pieces veal shank (about 8 ounces each), cut for osso buco
6	small pieces beef short ribs (about 4 ounces each)
6	chicken thighs, skinned
1	bay leaf
1	clove
8	parsley stems
1	cup dry white wine
2	cups chicken broth

FOR THE PESTO MAYONNAISE

2	cloves garlic, minced
¼	cup tightly packed fresh basil leaves, finely chopped
⅓	cup mayonnaise
2	tablespoons extra-virgin olive oil
2	tablespoon toasted pine nuts, finely chopped (see page 73)
2	tablespoons freshly grated Parmesan cheese
	Salt
	White pepper to taste

FOR THE SOUP

¾	cup cooked orzo, or other small pasta
1	plum tomato, skinned, seeded, and finely chopped
1	tablespoon chopped fresh Italian (flat-leaf) parsley

FOR THE MARROW TOASTS (OPTIONAL)

6	thick slices French bread, toasted
1	small lemon cut into 6 wedges

TO MAKE THE BOLLITO MISTO, place the onion, carrots, fennel ribs, and turnips in a 6-quart, or larger, slow cooker and sprinkle with salt and pepper to taste. Season the veal, beef, and chicken with salt and pepper and arrange on top of the vegetables. Nestle the bay leaf, clove, and parsley stems between the pieces of meat, and pour the wine and broth over all. Cover the cooker and cook for 6 to 8 hours on low, until the meat can be easily pierced with a fork.

WHILE THE BOLLITO MISTO IS COOKING, mix the ingredients for the pesto mayonnaise together in a medium bowl; cover and refrigerate.

WHEN THE BOLLITO MISTO IS DONE, carefully remove the meat and vegetables to a platter with a slotted spoon; keep warm.

TO MAKE THE SOUP, remove the bay leaf, clove, and parsley stems from the broth. Skim off the fat and correct the seasoning with salt and pepper to taste, if needed. Place a portion of cooked pasta, a portion of diced tomato, and a sprinkling of parsley in each of 6 soup bowls. Ladle the broth over the top and stir briefly to disperse the pasta and tomato; serve immediately.

TO SERVE the marrow toasts, if desired, scoop out the marrow from the centers of the veal shanks and serve with warm toast and a wedge of lemon as a middle course.

SERVE the meat and vegetables as a main course with pesto mayonnaise on the side.

Osso Buco Milanese

Although Milan is as hectic and harried as any modern city, its cuisine remains stubbornly slow. In the high-tech kitchens of high-rise apartments, pots of risotto linger on stove tops as they creep toward their inevitable creamy conclusion with the help of careful stirring. Casseroles of osso buco bubble in ovens, waiting for the meat to melt and the marrow to leach its richness into the simmering stew.

A continent away, in the land of twenty-minute dinners, we run from such recipes, not for health reasons or because we don't appreciate how they taste, but simply because they take "too long" to cook. And the faster we run, the more we lose. We lose the thrill of coaxing perfection from a shank of meat and a few diced vegetables. But with a slow cooker, more time doesn't mean more work. We can enjoy both convenience and the depth of flavor that only time can give to great food.

¼	cup flour
1	teaspoon kosher salt
½	teaspoon coarsely ground black pepper
4	veal shanks (about 1 pound each), cut 2 inches thick and tied securely around their perimeters
2	tablespoons extra-virgin olive oil
2	leeks (white part only), thoroughly washed, and cut into ¼-inch-thick slices
2	celery ribs, cut into ¼-inch dice
6	cloves garlic, minced, divided
½	cup dry white wine
1½	teaspoons dried thyme
1	teaspoon dried basil
1	cup chicken broth
2	cups canned diced tomatoes, drained
1	bay leaf
	Finely grated zest of 1 lemon
¼	cup finely chopped fresh Italian (flat-leaf) parsley

8

SERVINGS

PRECOOK
20 minutes

SLOW COOK
3 to 4 hours on high, or 6 to 8 hours on low, in a 5- to 6-quart slow cooker

MIX the flour, salt, and pepper in a medium bowl. Turn the veal shanks in the seasoned flour so that both flat sides are coated; pat off any excess and reserve the remaining flour mixture. Heat the oil in a large heavy skillet over medium-high heat, and brown the shanks on both sides, about 4 minutes per side. Transfer to a 5- to 6-quart slow cooker.

REDUCE the heat to medium. Add the leeks and celery and sauté until tender, about 4 minutes. Add half the garlic and the reserved seasoned flour and sauté for 30 seconds. Stir in the wine and bring to a boil. Add the thyme, basil, chicken broth, and tomatoes. Simmer, stirring, until slightly thickened, and pour over the shanks. Tuck the bay leaf between 2 shanks, cover the cooker, and cook for 3 to 4 hours on high, or 6 to 8 hours on low, until the meat can be pierced easily with a fork.

CONTINUED

Osso Buco Milanese CONTINUED

WHILE THE SHANKS ARE COOKING, combine the remaining garlic, the lemon zest, and parsley and set aside.

REMOVE the shanks to a platter, spoon off the fat from the surface off the liquid, and remove the bay leaf. Stir in half the garlic-lemon-parsley mixture. Remove the strings from the shanks, ladle the sauce over the meat, and scatter the remaining garlic-lemon-parsley mixture over top. Serve immediately.

Beef Carbonnade

Brittany is the England of France: pubs replace bistros, beer trumps wine, and carbonnade is their *boeuf bourguignonne*. Carbonnade takes advantage of the high moisture and sugar content of onions, simmering them until they collapse into a sweet, pungent syrup. Add a bottle of beer, the richness of well-exercised beef, some brown sugar, a few herbs, and several hours in a slow cooker, and you've got the heartiness of a British stew tweaked with a bit of je ne sais quoi.

4-6

SERVINGS

PRECOOK

30 minutes

SLOW COOK

4 to 5 hours on high, or 8 to 10 hours on low, in a 5- to 6-quart slow cooker

¼   **cup flour**

1   **teaspoon kosher salt**

½   **teaspoon coarsely ground black pepper**

3   **pounds beef chuck, trimmed of excess fat and tendon and cut into ¼-inch-thick slices**

3   **tablespoons extra-virgin olive oil**

5   **large onions, halved and cut into thin slices**

2   **slices salt pork or bacon, finely diced**

1   **tablespoon fines herbes, or heaping ½ teaspoon each thyme, oregano, sage, rosemary, and basil**

2   **teaspoons dark brown sugar**

1   **bottle (12 ounces) ale or lager beer**

2   **bay leaves**

2   **tablespoons fresh Italian (flat-leaf) parsley**

     Boiled noodles or potatoes (optional)

MIX the flour, salt, and pepper on a plate. Turn the beef in the seasoned flour so that both flat sides of the slices are coated; pat off any excess and reserve the remaining seasoned flour. Heat the oil in a large heavy skillet over medium-high heat and brown the beef slices in batches, 3 to 4 minutes per side. Set aside on a plate.

REDUCE heat to medium-low, add the onions, and cook until tender, about 10 minutes. Transfer to a 5- to 6-quart slow cooker and lay the beef on top.

ADD the salt pork to the skillet and cook over medium heat until cooked through but not crisp. Add the herbs and reserved seasoned flour and cook until the flour browns, about 3 minutes. Add the brown sugar and beer and simmer, stirring, until slightly thickened. Pour the sauce over the beef in the cooker. Bury the bay leaves in the sauce, cover, and cook on high for 4 to 5 hours, or on low for 8 to 10 hours. Remove the bay leaves.

REMOVE the beef to a serving platter. Stir the parsley into the sauce and spoon over the beef. Serve with boiled noodles or potatoes, if desired.

what else?

- Replace the lager with a dark beer for deeper color and a bittersweet edge.

- Carbonnade is also delicious made with beef short ribs.

Slow-Cooked Bouillabaisse

Fish stews exist wherever there's water. Some are as thin as soup and others are so chock-full of shellfish and fish that there is hardly enough room in the pot for broth. Bouillabaisse is a regional stew, and like all regional dishes, there are countless authentic recipes. You can drown in discussions over which ingredient list is the most correct, but you'll make a better bouillabaisse if you go straight to the heart of the matter. Prepare a delicious broth infused with the flavors of the region—fresh garlic, good olive oil, basil, fennel, saffron, citrus, and tomato—let it simmer until the flavors marry, add the freshest and brightest fish that's available, and then, whatever you do, don't overcook it. The broth can percolate for the better part of a day (or make it a day ahead); it will only get better. But once the seafood is added, timing is crucial. In a slow cooker set to high, this means no more than 15 to 20 minutes; check frequently near the end to make sure the chunks of fish are just about to flake, and the shrimp or scallops are barely resilient.

SERVINGS

PRECOOK
10 minutes

SLOW COOK
4 to 6 hours on low in a 3½-quart, or larger, slow cooker

AT THE END
20 minutes

½ teaspoon saffron threads

1 cup dry white wine

Juice and finely grated zest of ½ orange

2 tablespoons extra-virgin olive oil

1 large onion, diced

3 fennel ribs, diced

2 cloves garlic, minced

1 teaspoon dried basil

½ teaspoon dried thyme

½ teaspoon kosher salt

¼ teaspoon ground black pepper

4 cups fish stock, or 2 fish bouillon cubes (9 grams each) dissolved in 4 cups boiling water

1 can (about 15 ounces) diced tomatoes, drained

1 bay leaf

12 ounces boneless, skinless salmon fillet, cut into 1-inch pieces

12 ounces boneless, skinless lean fish fillet, such as cod, tilapia, or snapper, cut into 1-inch pieces

12 ounces (about 24) medium shrimp, peeled and deveined

Juice of ½ lemon

¼ cup fresh Italian (flat-leaf) parsley

IN A SMALL BOWL, crumble the saffron into the wine, stir in the orange juice, and set aside.

HEAT the oil in a large skillet over medium-high heat. Add the onion and fennel and sauté until the vegetables lose their raw look, about

CONTINUED

Slow-Cooked Bouillabaisse

3 minutes. Add the garlic, basil, thyme, salt, and pepper and sauté for 30 seconds. Add the wine-saffron mixture and bring to a boil. Add the fish stock, orange zest, tomatoes, and bay leaf and stir to combine.

POUR into a 3½-quart, or larger, slow cooker, cover the cooker, and cook on low for 4 to 6 hours.

ABOUT 30 MINUTES BEFORE SERVING, turn the cooker to high. Toss the salmon and shrimp with the lemon juice. Stir into the broth in the cooker, cover, and cook until the salmon cooks through, about 20 minutes. Stir in the parsley and ladle into bowls. Serve with plenty of crusty bread.

what else?

- The broth for bouillabaisse can be made days or weeks ahead and frozen. Just thaw it, bring it back to a boil, and add the fish.

- Feel free to vary the mix of fish and shellfish, but try to keep the proportions similar to the recipe's. In addition to (or in place of) salmon you could use any oily fish, such as swordfish, shark, tuna, or bluefish. Add scrubbed mussels or clams along with the shrimp, or replace the shrimp with lobster tail and/or scallops.

Game Hens Poêlée with Spring Vegetables

One could imagine a game hen, plump and petite, scurrying through the underbrush in a woodland. But in reality, it is nothing but a diminutive chicken, transformed here, through a classic technique for cooking small game birds, into something resembling that sylvan fantasy. Poêlée is a gentle form of roasting, but because the cooking is so slow, the effect is more like poaching in oil, making the transition to a slow cooker natural.

2   game hens (about 2 pounds each), split lengthwise and backbones removed

     Kosher salt

     Ground black pepper

6   tablespoons extra-virgin olive oil

1   cup (about 12) baby-cut carrots

2   cups (about 8) halved new potatoes

1   cup (about 16) frozen pearl onions

½   teaspoon dried thyme

½   teaspoon dried rosemary, crushed

2   cloves garlic, minced

1   cup (about 14) frozen artichoke hearts, quartered

¾   cup frozen peas, thawed

2   teaspoons chopped fresh tarragon

SERVINGS

PRECOOK

15 minutes

SLOW COOK

5 to 6 hours on low in a 5- to 6-quart slow cooker

AT THE END

2 minutes

SEASON the game hen halves with salt and pepper. Heat 2 tablespoons of the oil in a large skillet over medium heat. Brown the skin side of the hen halves until lightly browned, about 5 minutes; transfer to a plate and set aside.

ADD the carrots, potatoes, and pearl onions and sauté until lightly browned. Season with the thyme and rosemary and more salt and pepper; scrape into a 5- to 6-quart slow cooker. Place the game hen halves, skin side up, in a single layer on top of the vegetables.

ADD the garlic and artichoke hearts to the skillet and cook for a few minutes until lightly browned. Scatter over the game hens. Drizzle with the remaining 4 tablespoons oil. Cover the cooker and cook for 5 to 6 hours on low.

TO SERVE, transfer the hen halves to a platter. Stir the peas and tarragon into the other vegetables, and spoon around the hens. Spoon the juices remaining in the bottom of the cooker over the top and serve.

Vegetable Mains and Sides

VEGETABLES PROVIDE THE MOST FERTILE GROUND for slow cooker devotees and generally perform better than meats, which become desiccated when they simmer too long. Tough, fibrous vegetables just get creamier; meaty vegetables like mushrooms go plush; and stinky, sulfurous specimens like cauliflower and kohlrabi are tamed. The only vegetables that don't do well with long, slow cooking are greens, and these can be added at the end for a fresh jolt of color and flavor.

When slow-cooking vegetables of varying textures, you can offset their differences by cutting tougher vegetables into smaller chunks, and by layering longer-cooking vegetables toward the bottom of the crock and more tender vegetables nearer the top.

One of the great advantages of slow-cooking vegetables is the opportunity to infuse your ingredients with spices and other aromatics. Whole spices and herbs take time to release their magic, and even longer to work their way deep into the fibers of simmering ingredients. That's why slow cooking is the best way to infuse flavor into a vegetable curry. It's also the lazy man's preferred method for baked pastas, and the easiest way to roast beets.

CHAPTER 5

Recipes

Potatoes Parmesan

Potatoes go without notice. Consequently, we treat them as an afterthought, a sidekick to a steak or the filler in corned beef hash. But the deficiency lies in us, not the spud, for there is no other food that moves with such flawless grace from dish to dish and meal to meal. Potatoes are cheap, plentiful, and effortless to prepare, yet most of us never take advantage of their potential. Ignoring an international arsenal of potato recipes, we dig the rut of our cooking routines deeper by mindlessly repeating the same baked and boiled potato dishes endlessly. No more! This simple, hearty, savory gratin, simmered with garlic, rosemary, and Parmesan, will challenge any entree in your dinnertime lineup for star status.

SERVINGS

PRECOOK

15 minutes

SLOW COOK

3 to 4 hours on high, or 6 to 8 hours on low, in a 5- to 6-quart slow cooker

AT THE END

3 minutes

3 tablespoons olive oil

2 pounds russet potatoes, scrubbed and cut into 6 to 8 wedges each

1 medium onion, halved and cut into thin slices

3 cloves garlic, minced

1 teaspoon chopped fresh rosemary

1 teaspoon kosher salt

¼ teaspoon coarsely ground black pepper

1 tablespoon flour

1¼ cups chicken or vegetable broth

¼ cup finely grated Parmesan cheese

HEAT the oil in a large skillet over medium-high heat. Brown the cut sides of the potato wedges in the hot oil in batches, about 2 minutes per side; do not crowd the pan. Transfer the potatoes to a 5- to 6-quart slow cooker after browning.

ADD the onion to the oil in the skillet and cook over medium heat until tender, about 3 minutes. Add the garlic, rosemary, salt, pepper, and flour, and stir until the onion is evenly coated. Add the broth and simmer until it thickens slightly; pour over the potatoes. Cover with a folded kitchen towel, and top with the lid. Cook for 3 to 4 hours on high, or 6 to 8 hours on low, until the potatoes are tender.

REMOVE the towel, scatter the Parmesan over the top, cover, and cook for 3 minutes, or until the cheese melts.

what else?

- The dry, flaky texture of russet potatoes is desirable in this dish, but if you prefer a moister, creamier consistency, replace with 2 pounds of golden potatoes.

- Use any cheese you want. Try smoked Gouda, Gruyère, or an aged cheddar.

- Although I am especially fond of rosemary with potatoes, feel free to choose an herb to suit your taste. Thyme, parsley, and sage are all classic potato partners.

Barbecued Baked Beans

Barbecued beans take so much time and fiddling that most of us have long since abandoned home-made for canned. Well, I'm as fond of canned baked beans as the next guy, but I've never tasted any that can compare with the real thing. And when it comes to the real thing, you can't beat a slow cooker for ease and excellence. The cooking time is still absurdly long, the flavor is sweet, smoky, and spicy, and the texture is melt-in-your-mouth; all that's missing is the work. You can serve these beans as a side dish with grilled food, but to tell you the truth, there's enough smoked meat in the recipe to serve the beans with cornbread and call it a meal.

8

SERVINGS

PRECOOK

About 5 minutes plus 1 hour to overnight (depending on how you soak the beans)

SLOW COOK

10 to 12 hours on low, in a 4-quart, or larger, slow cooker

AT THE END

15 minutes

1	pound (2 cups) dried beans: white, pinto, or mixed
1	pound smoked ham hock or turkey leg
2	teaspoons vegetable oil
1	medium onion, diced

½	red bell pepper, seeded, ribbed, and diced
4	cups chicken broth
1	cup bottled spicy barbecue sauce, divided
½	teaspoon spicy chili powder

PUT the beans in a bowl, cover with at least 3 inches of water, and soak overnight. Or put the beans in a saucepan, cover with 3 inches of water, and bring to a boil. Cook at a boil for 3 minutes, remove from the heat, and let soak for 1 hour. Drain.

PLACE the smoked meat in a 4-quart, or larger, slow cooker and pour the soaked beans on top.

HEAT the oil in a large heavy skillet over medium-high heat. Add the onion and bell pepper and sauté until barely tender, about 3 minutes. Add the broth and bring to a boil. Remove from the heat and stir in ½ cup of the barbecue sauce; pour and scrape into the slow cooker, and mix to coat the beans. Cover the cooker and cook on low for 10 to 12 hours, until the beans are tender and the sauce is slightly thickened.

REMOVE the meat from the beans and set aside until cool enough to handle. Turn the cooker to high, mix the chili powder and remaining ½ cup barbecue sauce in a small bowl, and stir into the beans. Remove the skin and bone from the meat, and break the meat into small pieces. Stir into the beans and cook for 10 minutes.

SERVE immediately or keep warm for up to 2 hours.

what else?

- The type of bean you use will not affect the flavor of your baked beans, but it will alter the color slightly.

- If you want to make these beans vegetarian, you can eliminate the ham hock. Use a whole bell pepper, roasted and diced, instead of half a pepper, and replace the chicken broth with vegetable broth.

roasting bell peppers

Place a pepper directly onto the grate of a gas burner set on high, under a broiler set to the highest setting, or over a hot grill. As the skin on one side of the pepper burns, turn it over, and continue this way until the skin is uniformly burnt. Be careful to keep it moving so that the flesh under the skin doesn't char. Place the pepper in a paper bag or a bowl, close the bag or cover the bowl, and set aside until cool enough to handle. Peel off the burnt skin with your fingers, and remove the stems and seeds before dicing.

Grits for Breakfast, Lunch, or Dinner

"Grits," "mush," "polenta," "gruel," whatever you want to call it, it's easier to prepare in a slow cooker than by any other method. I love grits any way and any time of day, which is why this recipe aims at eternity. It starts with a basic recipe for stone-ground grits (mechanically ground grits come out mushy), and then amends it with peaches and pecans for breakfast, bacon and cheddar for lunch, and a ragoût of wild mushrooms for dinner. I don't advise you to eat all three in one day, but life could be worse.

FOR THE GRITS

2   quarts water

1   teaspoon kosher salt

¼   teaspoon ground black pepper

1   tablespoon butter

1½   cups stone-ground grits, yellow or white

FOR BREAKFAST, PEACHY PECAN GRITS

½   cup half-and-half

2   tablespoons light brown sugar

¼   teaspoon vanilla extract

1   peach, peeled, pitted, and finely chopped

½   cup chopped toasted pecans (see page 73)

FOR LUNCH, BACON-CHEDDAR GRITS

2   slices bacon, cooked until crisp and crumbled

⅔   cup shredded sharp cheddar cheese

FOR DINNER, SPINACH GRITS WITH WILD MUSHROOM RAGOÛT

2   tablespoons extra-virgin olive oil, divided

½   medium onion, chopped

8   ounces wild mushrooms, such as cremini, oyster, or shiitake, cut into slices

2   cloves garlic, minced

⅓   cup canned diced tomatoes, drained

½   cup chicken or vegetable broth

     Kosher salt

     Coarsely ground black pepper

2   tablespoons chopped fresh Italian (flat-leaf) parsley

1   bag (about 6 ounces) baby spinach, finely chopped

¼   cup grated Parmigiano-Reggiano cheese

SERVINGS

PRECOOK

10 minutes

SLOW COOK

3 to 4 hours on high, or 5 to 6 hours on low, in a 3- to 4-quart slow cooker

AT THE END

1 to 10 minutes

TO MAKE THE GRITS, bring the water to a boil in a medium saucepan over medium-high heat. Add the salt, pepper, and butter and stir until the butter melts. Add the grits in a slow, steady stream as you stir constantly with a whisk. Continue stirring until the grits return to a boil. Scrape into a 3- to 4-quart slow cooker. Cover the cooker and cook for 3 to 4 hours on high, or 5 to 6 hours on low, until creamy and thick.

CONTINUED

Grits for Breakfast, Lunch, or Dinner CONTINUED

TO MAKE PEACHY PECAN GRITS FOR BREAK-FAST, heat the half-and-half and brown sugar in a small saucepan over medium heat until the sugar dissolves. Remove from the heat and stir in the vanilla. Stir the sweetened cream into the cooked grits, along with the peach and pecans.

TO MAKE BACON-CHEDDAR GRITS FOR LUNCH, stir the bacon and cheese into the cooked grits and continue stirring until the cheese is half melted.

TO MAKE SPINACH GRITS WITH WILD MUSH-ROOM RAGOÛT FOR DINNER, heat 1 tablespoon of the olive oil in a large skillet over medium-high heat. Add the onion and sauté until barely tender, about 2 minutes. Add the mushrooms and sauté until browned, about 3 minutes. Add the garlic and cook another minute. Add the tomatoes, broth, salt, pepper, and parsley and simmer until the mushrooms are tender, about 3 minutes.

STIR the spinach, the remaining tablespoon of olive oil, and the cheese into the cooked grits and continue stirring until the spinach wilts. Serve the grits topped with the sautéed mushroom ragoût.

what else?

- Use any fruit for the breakfast grits: bananas, plums, and any berry are fine substitutions.

- If you want a vegetarian lunch, replace the bacon with a finely diced roasted red bell pepper.

- Leftover grits, once cooled, can be sliced and sautéed to serve as a side dish, or as a gravy sopper for stews and braised meats.

Curried Vegetables and Dal

The glory of curry is all in your nose. Close your eyes and you'll know what I mean. The blend of aromas aerating your head and the cacophony of sensations titillating your throat are as complex as any food in existence. It takes time and care to develop those flavors, and you'll find that the melting pot of a slow cooker gives you a delicious advantage. For the best flavor, start by toasting whole spices. Once ground, spices lose their potency, so starting with whole seeds yields the strongest impact. A brief sojourn in a hot dry skillet activates their aromatic oils, which are released after grinding, priming them to expand as they simmer throughout the day.

6-8

SERVINGS

PRECOOK

15 minutes

SLOW COOK

3 to 4 hours on high, or 6 to 8 hours on low, in a 5- to 6-quart slow cooker

AT THE END

15 minutes

2	teaspoons cumin seeds
1	teaspoon black coriander seeds
1	teaspoon coarsely ground black pepper
2	tablespoons olive oil
2	large onions, finely chopped
1	red bell pepper, stemmed, seeded, and cut into 1-inch pieces
1	green bell pepper, seeded, deribbed, and cut into 1-inch pieces
6	cloves garlic, minced
1	tablespoon minced gingerroot
1	teaspoon kosher salt

1	can (about 28 ounces) whole plum tomatoes, quartered, with their juice
1½	cups vegetable broth
1½	pounds acorn or butternut squash, peeled, seeded, and cut into 1½-inch cubes
12	ounces small potatoes, halved or quartered, depending on size
1½	cups red lentils, washed
1	cup coconut milk
	Pinch of red pepper flakes
¼	cup chopped fresh cilantro

HEAT a large heavy skillet (preferably cast-iron) over medium-high heat. Add the cumin, coriander, and black pepper and stir until the spices are very aromatic, about 1 minute; be careful not to burn them. Scrape the spices into a spice grinder, minichopper, or mortar and pestle and grind finely; set aside.

WIPE out the skillet, and heat the oil in it over medium-high heat. Add the onions, and red and green bell peppers and sauté until the vegetables are browned lightly, about 5 minutes. Add the reserved ground toasted spices, the garlic, ginger, and salt and sauté for 30 seconds. Stir in the tomatoes and vegetable broth, and heat to boiling.

LAYER the squash and potatoes in the bottom of a 5- to 6-quart slow cooker and scatter the lentils on top. Pour the contents of the skillet over all, cover the cooker, and cook for 3 to 4 hours on high, or 6 to 8 hours on low, until the vegetables and lentils are tender.

TURN the cooker to high, stir in the coconut milk and pepper flakes, and cook for 15 minutes. Serve the curry, garnished with the cilantro.

what else?

- If you want a lower-fat version, you can replace the coconut milk with yogurt and eliminate the last 15 minutes of cooking at the end.

Sweet Potatoes and Apples

The ingredients that are most successfully cooked in a slow cooker have two things in common—lots of fiber and lots of flavor. Sweet potatoes, anyone? Almost any sweet potato recipe can be adapted to the slow cooker, but this is one of my favorites. There is something magical about the combination of sweet potato and apple. The potato delivers a meaty heft and earthy flavor that lightens and brightens in the sweet-tart juice of a crisp apple. Although you could cook the apple completely in the slow cooker, I prefer sautéing it first. A little bit of browning adds a whole other dimension to the relationship.

4	dark-orange sweet potatoes (about 3 pounds), peeled and cut into 2-inch chunks
1	cup packed light brown sugar
1	teaspoon kosher salt
¼	teaspoon ground black pepper
½	teaspoon ground cinnamon
2	tablespoons butter, cut into small pieces, divided
1	large apple, such as Granny Smith, peeled, cored, and cut into ½-inch chunks

TOSS the potatoes, brown sugar, salt, pepper, and cinnamon in a 3- to 4-quart slow cooker. Dot the top with half the butter. Cover the cooker with a folded kitchen towel and top with the lid. Cook for 3 to 4 hours on high, or 6 to 8 hours on low, until the potatoes are tender.

WHILE THE SWEET POTATOES ARE COOKING, heat the remaining butter in a medium skillet over medium heat. Add the apples and sauté until lightly browned and tender, about 5 minutes; set aside.

WHEN THE POTATOES ARE TENDER, add the apples to the potatoes. Drain as much liquid from the cooker as you can into the skillet used for sautéing the apples. Cook over medium-high heat for 2 to 3 minutes, until slightly thickened. Toss with the apples and potatoes, and serve.

6

SERVINGS

PRECOOK
5 minutes

SLOW COOK
3 to 4 hours on high, or 6 to 8 hours on low, in a 3- to 4-quart slow cooker

AT THE END
10 minutes

Caponata

Along the Mediterranean, salads are rarely raw. Instead, the region is known for ratatouille, marinated mushrooms, roasted peppers, fava beans, olives, and the king of them all, caponata—the raucous sautéed salad of Sicily, composed of eggplant, onions, peppers, garlic, anchovies, olives, capers, and lots of extra-virgin olive oil. It struck me that using a slow cooker might be an effortless way to mix up a batch, and the results were chunky, creamy, and rich. Start by sautéing the vegetables just enough to tinge them with color. Leave them to simmer, and finish with piquant ingredients that don't need cooking, like olives and capers. You can serve caponata as a side dish, a first course, or on bread. It is most often eaten at room temperature, but I don't pay too much attention to that and find it equally good warm or chilled.

SERVINGS

PRECOOK

15 minutes

SLOW COOK

2 to 3 hours on high, or 4 to 6 hours on low, in a 3- to 4-quart slow cooker

AT THE END

15 minutes resting

¼ cup extra-virgin olive oil, divided

2 firm medium eggplants, stemmed and diced

1⅓ cups diced celery

1⅓ cups chopped onion

1 large green bell pepper, seeded, deribbed, and diced

2 cloves garlic, finely chopped

2 teaspoons dried basil

½ teaspoon dried oregano

2 cups canned diced tomatoes, with their juice

1 teaspoon kosher salt

¼ teaspoon coarsely ground black pepper

3 tablespoons red wine vinegar

1 tablespoon minced anchovies or anchovy paste

⅓ cup chopped green olives

1½ tablespoon small capers (nonpareils)

3 tablespoons chopped fresh Italian (flat-leaf) parsley

HEAT 2 tablespoons of the olive oil in a large skillet over medium-high heat. Add the eggplants, in batches, and cook until browned, about 4 minutes per batch. Transfer to a 3- to 4-quart slow cooker.

ADD 1 tablespoon of the olive oil to the skillet. Add the celery, onion, and bell pepper and sauté until tender, about 3 minutes. Add the garlic, basil, and oregano and stir to combine.

Add the tomatoes, salt, pepper, and vinegar and heat to boiling. Stir into the slow cooker, cover, and cook for 2 to 3 hours on high, or 4 to 6 hours on low, until the vegetables are tender.

STIR in the remaining olive oil, the anchovies, olives, capers, and parsley, and transfer to a serving bowl. Serve warm, at room temperature, or chilled, either as an appetizer with crusty bread or as a side dish.

Chèvre and Pumpkin Lasagna

In Italy, pumpkin is thought of as a vegetable. Instead of loading it up with sugar and cinnamon, Italians invigorate it with garlic and cheese, and if it is sweetened at all, the sugar derives naturally from an addition of caramelized onions or roasted leeks. That is the charm of this easy and elegant lasagna, in which leaves of pasta are layered with creamy, cheesy pumpkin custard, a rich and tangy relish of sautéed onions, and nubbins of fresh goat cheese. Serve it as a luxurious first course or a sinful vegetarian entrée.

8

SERVINGS

PRECOOK

30 minutes

SLOW COOK

3 to 4 hours on low
in a 5- to 6-quart
slow cooker

AT THE END

10 minutes

3   tablespoons extra-virgin olive oil, divided

3   large onions, halved and cut into thin slices

4   cloves garlic, minced, divided

1½ teaspoons kosher salt, divided

¾   teaspoon coarsely ground black pepper, divided

1   teaspoon dried ground sage

1   teaspoon dried thyme

1   tablespoon flour

1½ cups vegetable broth

2   tablespoons aged balsamic vinegar

¼   cup chopped fresh Italian (flat-leaf) parsley, divided

1   can (about 15 ounces) 100% pumpkin puree

2   large eggs

¼   cup seasoned breadcrumbs

⅓   cup finely chopped pine nuts

¾   cup freshly grated Parmesan cheese, divided

12 lasagna noodles, cooked according to the package directions and cooled in cold water

8   ounces fresh chèvre (goat cheese), broken into small pieces

HEAT 2 tablespoons of the olive oil in a large skillet over medium heat. Add the onions and cook slowly until lightly browned, about 10 minutes. Add three-fourths of the garlic, 1 teaspoon of the salt, ½ teaspoon of the pepper, the sage, thyme, and flour and stir until the onions are thoroughly coated. Cook for 1 minute, stirring constantly. Add the broth and stir until slightly thickened. Stir in the vinegar and half the parsley and set aside.

MIX the pumpkin, eggs, breadcrumbs, pine nuts, ½ cup of the Parmesan, and the remaining parsley, and garlic, the ¼ teaspoon salt, and 1 teaspoon pepper in a medium mixing bowl.

COAT the interior of the crock of a 5- to 6-quart slow cooker with the remaining tablespoon of olive oil. Spoon a fourth of the onion mixture over the bottom of the crock, top with 3 lasagna noodles, a third of the pumpkin mixture, and a third of the chèvre. Spoon a third of the remaining onion mixture over the chèvre, top with 3 more noodles, half the remaining pumpkin, and half the remaining chèvre. Spoon half the remaining onion mixture over the chèvre, top with 3 more noodles, the remaining pumpkin, the remaining chèvre, and the remaining onion mixture. Cover with the 3 remaining noodles. Cover the crock with 2 kitchen towels and the lid. Cook for 3 to 4 hours on low. When the lasagna is done, the edges will be browned and the center will be barely set.

TOP with the remaining ¼ cup of the Parmesan cheese and cover until melted, about 1 minute. Remove the crock from the cooker and let rest for about 10 minutes before serving. Cut into 8 portions and serve.

Mushroom-Barley Risotto

I have tried many recipes for slow cooker risotto, and I have reached the conclusion that they just don't work. Yes, you get something resembling cheesy, gooey rice, but the convenience does not make up for the loss of sensual perfection that real risotto cooked on a stove top embodies. The fall from grace, for me at least, is too much to bear. With that in mind, I would like to introduce you to barley risotto. Unlike rice, barley gets creamy, rather than gluey, during long, slow simmering. The finished dish is like a savory pudding, overflowing with rich dairy textures, cheesy aromas, and meaty chunks of mushrooms. Serve it as a first course in an elaborate dinner, or as a special side dish to accompany roasted meat or poultry.

6–8

SERVINGS

PRECOOK

10 minutes

SLOW COOK

3 to 4 hours on high
in a 5- to 6-quart
slow cooker

AT THE END

2 minutes

1	tablespoon extra-virgin olive oil
1	onion, finely chopped
8	medium white mushrooms, trimmed and cut into slices
2	cloves garlic, minced
2	cups pearl barley
1	cup dry white wine
4	cups chicken or mushroom broth

1	teaspoon kosher salt
¼	teaspoon coarsely ground black pepper
½	ounce dried porcini mushrooms, crumbled (¼ cup)
1	teaspoon chopped fresh rosemary
½	cup freshly grated Parmesan cheese
½	cup cream or half-and-half
1	tablespoon chopped fresh Italian (flat-leaf) parsley

HEAT the oil in a large skillet over medium heat. Add the onion and mushrooms and sauté until tender, about 4 minutes. Add the garlic and barley and sauté for 1 minute, stirring constantly. Add the wine and stir until almost completely absorbed. Transfer to a 5- to 6-quart slow cooker.

ADD the broth, salt, pepper, dried porcini, and rosemary to the slow cooker and stir to moisten the barley. Cover the crock with a folded towel, and top with the lid. Cook for 3 to 4 hours on high, until the barley is tender.

STIR in the Parmesan, cream, and parsley, and fluff with a fork until the cheese melts and the barley is moistened. Serve immediately.

what else?

- If you like more assertive cheeses, use a combination of Romano cheese and Parmesan instead of all Parmesan, or replace half the cream with 2 ounces creamy fresh chèvre.

- You can replace the white mushrooms with something more exotic, like cremini, or go wild with fresh porcinis, cèpes, or morels.

- Although I would usually say you can use any dried wild mushroom in a recipe, I encourage you stick to porcini here; their flavor is wonderful with the mild sweetness of barley.

Cannellini Cannelloni with Wild Mushroom Gravy

Pasta e fagiole, the inspired combo of white beans and macaroni, is the soul food of Tuscany, and though many Americans may balk at its unapologetic heft, it is one of the world's great stick-to-your-ribs dishes. It is also the inspiration for these elegant cannelloni, stuffed with a mixture of cannellini beans, ricotta cheese, and garlic, and layered with tomato sauce loaded with wild mushrooms. It is ovo-lacto vegetarian and utterly rich; serving it with more than a side salad or some sautéed spinach would be overkill. Anyone who can't say "cannellini cannelloni" fast three times gets stuck doing the dishes.

SERVINGS

PRECOOK

20 minutes

SLOW COOK

3 to 4 hours on high, or 6 to 7 hours on low, in a 5- to 6-quart slow cooker

AT THE END

10 minutes

FOR THE FILLING

2   cans (about 15 ounces each) cannellini beans, drained and rinsed

3   tablespoons extra-virgin olive oil

3   cloves garlic, minced

⅓   cup ricotta cheese, preferably whole-milk

⅓   cup freshly grated Parmesan cheese

1   extra-large egg

1   teaspoon kosher salt

½   teaspoon ground black pepper

FOR THE SAUCE

2   tablespoons extra-virgin olive oil

1   pound cremini, shiitake, or other "wild" mushrooms, sliced

2   cloves garlic, minced

1   cup vegetable broth

3   cups tomato pasta sauce

FOR ASSEMBLY

1   tablespoon extra-virgin olive oil

12   oven-ready or no-boil cannelloni shells

⅓   cup freshly grated Parmesan cheese

TO MAKE THE FILLING, mash the beans with a potato masher or ricer. Heat the 3 tablespoons oil in a small skillet over medium-high heat. Add the 3 cloves garlic and the mashed beans and mix until everything is well blended and the beans are bubbling around the edges, about 1 minute. Transfer the bean mixture to a small bowl and stir in the ricotta, Parmesan, egg, salt, and pepper and set aside.

TO MAKE THE SAUCE, heat the 2 tablespoons olive oil in a large saucepan over medium heat. Add the mushrooms and 2 cloves garlic and sauté until the mushrooms are tender, about 5 minutes. Add the vegetable broth and tomato pasta sauce and heat until simmering; set aside.

TO ASSEMBLE, coat the interior of a 5- to 6-quart slow cooker with olive oil, and spoon 1 cup sauce over the bottom of a 5- to 6-quart slow cooker. Spoon the bean mixture into the cannelloni shells from either end, shaking them slightly to make sure they are filled all the way through the center. Arrange half of them in a single layer over the sauce. Top with another cup of sauce, and arrange the remaining shells in a second layer. Top with remaining sauce, cover the cooker, and cook for 3 to 4 hours on high, or 6 to 7 hours on low, until bubbling around the edges and heated through.

SCATTER the ⅓ cup Parmesan cheese over the cannelloni and cook on high for 10 minutes more.

what else?

- If you can't find oven-ready cannelloni shells, you can use the traditional kind that require boiling, but you will have to boil them before filling, for about 2 minutes less than the time indicated on the package.

- It is only possible to fit 6 cannelloni in a single layer in a typical 5- to 6-quart slow cooker, but if you have a casserole model, which has a flat, wide crockery insert (similar to a 9-by-13-inch baking pan), you will be able to cook all 12 cannelloni in a single layer, which makes serving neater.

Vegetable Tagine

A *tagine* is both a Moroccan shallow clay pot with a conical lid and any slow-cooked stew simmered in it. The most similar cooking device found in a modern American kitchen is a slow cooker, and since the essence of any tagine is its seductively flavored broth, it is possible to produce a fairly authentic Moroccan tagine in a slow cooker with the right ingredients. A tagine can be made of any meat or vegetable, but the spices are fairly uniform: chiles, thyme, turmeric, coriander, cumin, and cinnamon. Serve this, or any tagine, with lots of bread to sop up every droplet of sauce, as is customary in Morocco.

2   tablespoons extra-virgin olive oil

2   leeks, (white and light green parts only), thoroughly washed, and cut into ½-inch-thick slices

1   small rutabaga (about 8 ounces), peeled and cut into ¾-inch dice

2   carrots, peeled and cut into ¼-inch-thick slices

2   parsnips, peeled and cut into ¼-inch-thick slices

2   celery ribs, cut into ½-inch-thick slices

2   tablespoons minced gingerroot

4   cloves garlic, minced

1   teaspoon ground turmeric

1   tablespoon fresh thyme leaves

1   teaspoon kosher salt

½   teaspoon coarsely ground black pepper

1   teaspoon ground coriander

½   teaspoon ground cumin, preferably ground from whole seeds toasted in a dry skillet

1   can (about 28 ounces) diced tomatoes, preferably fire roasted, with their juice

1   can (about 15 ounces) chickpeas, drained and rinsed

1   large butternut squash (about 2 pounds), stemmed, peeled, seeded, and cut into 2-inch chunks

1   stick cinnamon

1   tablespoon honey

1   tablespoon fresh lemon juice

1   teaspoon hot pepper sauce

2   tablespoons finely chopped fresh cilantro

8

SERVINGS

PRECOOK

15 minutes

SLOW COOK

4 to 5 hours on high, or 7 to 8 hours on low, in a 5- to 6-quart slow cooker

AT THE END

2 minutes

HEAT the oil in a large deep skillet over medium-high heat. Add the leeks, rutabaga, carrots, parsnips, and celery and sauté until the carrots are barely tender, about 4 minutes. Add the ginger, garlic, turmeric, thyme, salt, pepper, coriander, and cumin and stir to disperse; cook for 1 minute. Add the tomatoes and chickpeas and heat to boiling; set aside.

PUT the butternut squash in a 5- to 6-quart slow cooker. Pour the contents of the skillet over the top, and submerge the cinnamon stick in the sauce. Cover the cooker and cook for 4 to 5 hours on high, or 7 to 8 hours on low.

WHILE THE TAGINE COOKS, mix the honey, lemon juice, and hot pepper sauce in a small bowl. When the tagine is done, remove the cinnamon stick, drizzle the honey mixture over top, and toss gently to disperse. Scatter the cilantro over the top and serve.

Slow-Roasted Beets
with Walnut Gremolata

Roasted beets are as different from their ubiquitous boiled brethren as cherry gelatin is from real cherries. Where boiled beets are bitter and mushy, roasted beets are all sweet and meaty. The challenge to roasting them is that they take time and attention. You can't walk away because they are likely to bake dry, and it takes a considerable amount of testing and poking to judge their doneness. The slow cooker fixes that. Because slow cookers hold in moisture, they can bake beets without any danger of scorching or dehydration. These beets are baked with orange juice and garlic, and finished with a crunchy fresh relish of walnuts, garlic, parsley, and bits of orange zest. Serve them with any roasted meat or grilled fish.

6	large beets (about 2 pounds), stems and leaves trimmed, scrubbed	¾	teaspoon kosher salt, divided
2	tablespoons water	¼	teaspoon coarsely ground black pepper
¼	cup orange juice	½	cup walnut pieces
1	tablespoon extra-virgin olive oil		Finely grated zest of ½ orange
1	large clove garlic, quartered, divided	1	tablespoon finely chopped fresh Italian (flat-leaf) parsley

ARRANGE the beets in a single layer in a microwave-safe shallow dish. Add the water, cover with microwave-safe plastic wrap, and cook in a microwave at full power for 8 minutes. The beets will be hot and barely cooked; this step makes it easier to peel them without losing a lot of their juice.

HOLD under cold running water until the beets are cool enough to handle. Trim off the tough stem ends of the beets, peel with a vegetable peeler, and cut the beets into quarters. Put in a 5- to 6-quart slow cooker.

MIX the orange juice, oil, half of the garlic, ½ teaspoon of the salt, and the pepper in a small bowl. Pour over the beets and toss to coat. Cover the cooker and cook for 2 to 3 hours on high, or 4 to 5 hours on low, until the beets are fork-tender.

SERVINGS

PRECOOK

15 minutes

SLOW COOK

2 to 3 hours on high, or 4 to 5 hours on low, in a 5- to 6-quart slow cooker

CONTINUED

Slow-Roasted Beets
with Walnut Gremolata CONTINUED

WHILE THE BEETS ARE COOKING, toast the walnuts in a small dry skillet over medium heat, stirring constantly, until lightly browned and aromatic, about 4 minutes. Cool briefly and chop finely. Chop the remaining garlic and mix with the walnuts, orange zest, the remaining ¼ teaspoon salt, and the parsley; set aside.

REMOVE the beets from the cooker with a slotted spoon and place in a serving bowl. Sprinkle the walnut gremolata on top and serve.

what else?

- Although red beets are the most commonly available, feel free to use other colors like golden or Chioggia (red and white striped). Don't mix these with dark red beets, however, because they will turn everything red.

176

Potato and Cauliflower Masala

Aloo gobhi, the classic Punjabi combination of spiced cauliflower and potato, is the inspiration for this vegan stew of hearty vegetables infused with Indian spices. Serve it as a side dish with roasted or grilled meats, or as a vegetarian main course accompanied by rice pilaf or warm flatbreads.

3 tablespoons vegetable oil, divided

1 teaspoon cumin seeds

½ teaspoon black mustard seeds

2 pounds golden potatoes, peeled and cut into 1-inch dice

1 large cauliflower, trimmed and broken into large florets

1 tablespoon minced gingerroot

1 can (about 15 ounces) diced tomatoes, with their liquid

½ teaspoon ground turmeric

2 teaspoon ground coriander

½ teaspoon garam masala

1 teaspoon light brown sugar

1 teaspoon kosher salt

1 jalapeño pepper, stemmed, seeded, and finely chopped

Juice of ½ lime

3 tablespoons chopped fresh cilantro

HEAT 2 tablespoons of the oil in a large heavy skillet over medium-high heat. Add the cumin and mustard seeds and cook until the mustard seeds turn gray and start to pop, about 30 seconds. Add the potatoes and sauté until spotted with brown, about 5 minutes. Transfer to a 4-quart, or larger, slow cooker.

ADD the remaining tablespoon of oil and the cauliflower to the skillet and sauté until spotted with brown, about 4 minutes. Transfer to the cooker.

ADD the ginger, tomatoes, turmeric, coriander, garam masala, brown sugar, and salt to the skillet and simmer for 1 minute. Pour over the vegetables, cover the cooker, and cook for 3 to 4 hours on high, or 5 to 6 hours on low, until the vegetables are tender.

ADD the jalapeño and lime juice, toss gently, and cook on high for 10 minutes. Scatter with cilantro and serve.

SERVINGS

Makes 4 entrees or 6 side dishes

PRECOOK

15 minutes

SLOW COOK

3 to 4 hours on high, or 5 to 6 hours on low, in a 4-quart, or larger, slow cooker

AT THE END

10 minutes

Fennel Braised with Artichokes

Elegance is not usually a key attribute of vegetables. We speak of them as healthy, colorful, and flavorful, but their ability to transport a plate toward unabashed sophistication is rare. (I know there are truffles, but who in his right mind is going to slow-cook a truffle?) This dish has that power, thanks to its seductive marriage of two Mediterranean vegetables. The preparation is no more complicated than an average sauté, but the flavors and textures may cause swooning; consider yourself warned.

¼   cup extra-virgin olive oil, divided

2   fennel bulbs, stems and leaves trimmed and bulbs cut lengthwise into ½-inch-thick slices

1   medium onion, halved and cut into slices

4   cloves garlic, finely chopped

1   teaspoon chopped fresh rosemary

½   teaspoon dried oregano

¼   teaspoon dried thyme

½   teaspoon kosher salt

¼   teaspoon coarsely ground black pepper

1   tablespoon flour

½   cup dry white wine

¾   cup vegetable or chicken broth

½   cup canned diced tomatoes, drained

1   can (about 15 ounces) artichoke hearts, drained and quartered

3   tablespoon chopped fresh Italian (flat-leaf) parsley

HEAT half the oil in a large deep skillet over medium-high heat. Brown the fennel slices in the oil on both sides, about 2 minutes per side, and transfer to a plate.

ADD the onion to the skillet and sauté over medium heat until tender, about 3 minutes. Add the garlic, rosemary, oregano, thyme, salt, and pepper and sauté for 30 seconds. Stir in the flour until the onions are coated. Add the wine and heat to boiling. Add the broth and tomatoes and stir until boiling.

COAT a 3- to 4-quart slow cooker with the remaining oil. Layer half the fennel slices in the cooker, cover with half the artichoke quarters, and then half the sauce. Repeat the layers. Cover the cooker and cook for 3 to 4 hours on high, or 6 to 8 hours on low, until everything is tender. Scatter parsley over the top and serve.

4

SERVINGS

PRECOOK

15 minutes

SLOW COOK

3 to 4 hours on high, or 6 to 8 hours on low, in a 3- to 4-quart slow cooker

---

2/21/14 - SO DELICIOUS

ate over baguette w/ side salad & was plenty for 2 people, double if having 4. Cooked on the long side & veggies really broke down, so maybe err on the shorter time next time.

Blue Cheese–Walnut Cheesecake

There is no law that says cheesecake must be sweet. Like pie, pancakes, or popcorn, it is little more than a vehicle for flavor. Think of this pungent, savory cheesecake as the cheese ball for the next decade. It takes no precooking and can be assembled in less than 10 minutes. You will need a 1½-quart soufflé dish that fits comfortably inside a large slow cooker. The one I use has a 6½-inch diameter, which fits perfectly into a 5- to 6-quart cooker. (I have another that's 7 inches across, and it won't fit in any of my slow cookers.) Serve the cheesecake, chilled, as an hors d'oeuvre, accompanied by fruit and bread. It is perfect for a large gathering. This recipe will yield 16 good-size wedges, but when folks are milling about, taking a sliver here and there, it could serve twice that many people.

16

SERVINGS

PRECOOK

15 minutes

SLOW COOK

6 to 10 hours on low in a 1½-quart soufflé dish set inside a 6-quart, or larger, slow cooker

AT THE END

4 hours, or longer, cooling

Nonstick oil spray	2 **tablespoons whiskey, Scotch or Irish**
¼ **cup ground walnuts (walnut meal)**	8 **ounces blue cheese, crumbled**
1 **medium onion, diced**	1 **teaspoon kosher salt**
1 **clove garlic, halved**	½ **teaspoon ground black pepper**
1 **pound cream cheese, regular or lite (not fat free), at room temperature**	4 **extra-large eggs**
1½ **tablespoons red wine vinegar**	1 **cup finely chopped toasted walnuts (see page 73)**

SPRAY a 1½-quart soufflé dish (6 inches in diameter at its base) with oil, dust with the ground walnuts, and set aside.

PURÉE the onion and garlic in a large food processor. Add the cream cheese, vinegar, whiskey, blue cheese, salt, and pepper and purée until smooth. Add the eggs and process again until smooth, scraping down the sides of the work bowl as needed. Add the walnuts and process just long enough to incorporate.

POUR into the prepared soufflé dish. Cut a round of parchment paper or wax paper just large enough to fit the top. Spray with oil and place, oil side down, on top of the batter. Cover the top with a sheet of heavy aluminum foil, crimping the edges to secure it tightly. Set the soufflé dish on a long sheet of foil and wrap over the top, completely enclosing the dish in foil. Place the dish in the center of a 6-quart, or larger, slow cooker. Pour boiling water into the cooker so that it comes 1½ inches up the sides of the dish. Cover the cooker and cook for 6 to 10 hours on low.

REMOVE the dish and unwrap; place on a rack until it cools to room temperature. Cover with plastic, invert onto a plate, and remove the dish. Invert onto a serving plate and refrigerate for at least 3 hours, or for several days.

SERVE in slices with toasts and/or pears or grapes.

Sweet and Slow

SWEETS ARE FOODS SET APART. Unfettered by the constraints of nutritional sensibility or the need to fit into a meal, sweets invite you to let your desires run free. Slow cooking and indulgence don't frequently go together, but that doesn't mean they can't join forces. The moist, gentle environment inside the inner reaches of a slow cooker is just the place to steam a pudding, relax a peck of apples into applesauce, or brown a betty.

You can even bake cakes in a slow cooker, provided they are moist and rich recipes, by using a baking pan that fits inside the crock insert. I have found that a 6-cup soufflé dish with a diameter of less than 7 inches fits in most slow cookers 6 quarts or larger. You could also use a 1-quart baking dish or a 6-inch baking pan, though these are hard to come by.

In most recipes, the crock is filled with enough water to come 1 inch up the side of the baking pan. The water helps to ensure that the temperature at the surface of the baking pan doesn't get hotter than 212°F, which is important for delicate puddings and custards. At other times (for a fruit cake, for instance), the baking pan just sits in the cooker and bakes as it would in an oven. In either case you will want to cover the top of the cooker with a folded kitchen towel to absorb steam and prevent it from dripping back onto the surface of the dessert.

6

Recipes

Chocolate Pudding Cake

A pudding cake is a definitively American, decidedly homey dessert, in which a cake batter is topped with some sort of syrup and then baked. In the alchemical atmosphere of the slow cooker, the cake part rises up through the syrup, or maybe it's the syrup that sinks down through the cake. But at any rate, the exchange produces a moist, brownie-like cake resting on a swamp of chocolate pudding. To serve it, scoop up some cake with its pudding foundation and eat it with a spoon.

Nonstick oil spray

1 **cup flour**

2 **teaspoons baking powder**

¼ **teaspoon salt**

1 **cup granulated sugar, divided**

½ **cup unsweetened cocoa powder, divided**

½ **cup milk**

1 **teaspoon vanilla extract**

¼ **cup vegetable oil**

½ **cup dark brown sugar**

1 **cup boiling water or coffee**

SPRAY a 1½-quart soufflé dish with oil and set aside.

COMBINE the flour, baking powder, salt, ¾ cup of the granulated sugar, and ¼ cup of the cocoa in a mixing bowl. Add the milk, vanilla, and oil and mix into a stiff batter. Scrape into the prepared dish and smooth the top.

MIX the brown sugar, the remaining ¼ cup granulated sugar, and remaining ¼ cup cocoa in a small bowl; sprinkle in an even layer over the top of the batter. Pour the boiling water or coffee over all. Set the dish inside a 6-quart slow cooker and cover the top of the slow cooker with a folded kitchen towel, and then with the cooker lid. Cook on high for 2½ hours, or until the top of the cake is set and the bottom is still syrupy.

CUT into wedges or spoon onto plates, using the syrup on the bottom as a sauce.

6

SERVINGS

PRECOOK
15 minutes

SLOW COOK
2½ hours on high
in a 1½-quart soufflé
dish set into a 6-quart,
or larger, slow cooker

what else?

- For a more grown-up version, replace half the boiling water or coffee with liquor, such as brandy.

Slow-Cooked Banana Bread Pudding

Soft and pudgy, cozy and unchallenging, sweet and a tad plain—these might not describe an ideal date, but when you're talking about bread pudding, nothing could sound more attractive. I love bread pudding so much that I have almost stopped making it, lest I balloon into a bread pudding myself. So it was with special appreciation that I dove into this creation as it emerged from my slow cooker. The subtle, steady warmth of a slow cooker is ideal for puddings, which have a tendency to curdle if they get too hot or cook too fast. However, they also mustn't cook too long, which means you will need a slow cooker that will automatically switch to warm at 3 hours, or you will have to make it on a day when you can be around to monitor it. The pudding will reward your vigilance with mild weight gain and extreme contentment.

6-8

SERVINGS

PRECOOK

20 minutes plus
20 minutes resting

SLOW COOK

2 to 3 hours on high
in a 1½-quart soufflé
dish set into a 6-quart,
or larger, slow cooker

AT THE END

4 to 5 minutes

---

1   tablespoon unsalted butter, cut into small pieces, divided

2   ripe bananas, finely chopped

¾   cup sugar, divided

7   slices firm bread, white or whole-wheat, cut into 1-inch squares

2   cups milk

½   teaspoon vanilla extract
     Pinch of salt

2   large or extra-large eggs

⅛   teaspoon ground nutmeg

¼   teaspoon ground cinnamon

HEAT 1 teaspoon of the butter in a medium saucepan over medium heat. Add the bananas and cook until they begin to soften, about 1 minute. Add 1 tablespoon of the sugar and cook until it dissolves. Toss the bananas and bread together in a mixing bowl and mound in a 1½-quart soufflé dish; set aside.

ADD the milk to the saucepan and heat over medium heat, stirring often, until bubbles form around the edges of the pan. Stir ½ cup of the remaining sugar into the milk and continue stirring until it dissolves. Stir in the vanilla and salt, remove from the heat, and let rest for 5 minutes.

WHISK together about a third of the milk mixture and the eggs in a small bowl. Then stir the mixture back into the remaining milk. Pour over the bread and bananas. Cover with a sheet of plastic wrap, and place a saucer small enough to fit inside the rim of the soufflé dish on top of the bread. If the weight of the saucer is not sufficient to submerge the bread beneath the surface of the milk, put another saucer on top. Set aside for about 20 minutes, until the bread has soaked up most of the milk. Remove the saucer(s) and the plastic wrap.

MEANWHILE mix the nutmeg and cinnamon with the remaining 3 tablespoons sugar in a small bowl and sprinkle over the surface of the pudding. Dot the top of the pudding with the remaining butter and cover the top loosely with foil. Place inside a 6-quart, or larger, slow cooker and pour enough boiling water into the crock around the soufflé dish to reach 1 inch up the sides of the soufflé dish. Cover the top of the cooker with a folded kitchen towel and top with the lid. Cook for 2 to 3 hours on high, until a tester inserted in the center comes out with just a few specks clinging to it. Remove the pudding from the cooker and cool for at least 10 minutes or to room temperature.

PREHEAT a broiler, and place the pudding under the broiler about 6 inches from the heat. Broil until the top browns lightly, 4 to 5 minutes. Serve warm or at room temperature.

what else?

- Feel free to replace the bananas with a large peach, peeled and diced, or a large apple or pear, peeled, cored, and diced.

- I like bread pudding served spartanly, but I have many friends, more decadent than me, who prefer to douse theirs with liquor and crown it with whipped cream. This banana pudding is delicious drizzled with a spoonful of warm rum or brandy, or served with a scoop of caramel ice cream.

Chunky Applesauce

If you've never had homemade applesauce or have been eating from the jar for so long that the memory of the real thing has vanished, I encourage you to use your slow cooker as a vehicle for discovery. I've employed two kinds of apples in this recipe: McIntosh, which melts into a thick, creamy sauce, and Granny Smith, which remains stubbornly solid. Together they yield a beautifully thick applesauce punctuated with voluptuous chunks.

8

SERVINGS
(2 quarts)

PRECOOK
10 minutes

SLOW COOK
3 hours on high,
or 6 hours on low,
in a 5- to 6-quart
slow cooker

AT THE END
2 minutes

1	teaspoon apple cider vinegar
1	gallon water
8	large McIntosh apples
4	medium Granny Smith apples

2 to 4	tablespoons sugar
¼	teaspoon ground cinnamon (optional)

MIX the vinegar and water in a large mixing bowl. Peel the apples and put them into the vinegar water as soon as they are peeled. Cut the apples in half from top to bottom, scoop out the core from each half with a melon baller, and toss the apples back into the vinegar water as soon as each is cut and cored. When finished coring, remove the apples with a slotted spoon and cut into 1- to 2-inch chunks. Toss in a 5- to 6-quart slow cooker with 2 tablespoons of the sugar. Cover the cooker and cook for 3 hours on high, or for 6 hours on low, until the apples are tender.

STIR the apples with a large spoon; they will immediately form a chunky sauce. Add the cinnamon, if desired, and as much of the remaining sugar as you like. Serve warm or chilled. Store, tightly closed, in the refrigerator for up to 5 days.

what else?

- As noted earlier, McIntosh apples make the thickest, creamiest applesauce, but you can substitute many other apples, like Golden Delicious, Gala, Fuji, or Jonathans. However, I recommend that you always use at least half McIntosh.

- You can also make a vanilla pear sauce using this recipe and substituting Bartlett pears for the McIntosh apples and Bosc for the Granny Smith. Replace the cider vinegar with lemon juice, and the cinnamon with vanilla extract.

Slow "Baked" Pears and Apples

When it comes to baking fruit, a slow cooker is not the same as a conventional oven. For one thing, in slow cooking, the baking dish and the oven walls are one, which means that there is nowhere for evaporating liquid seeping from the fruit to go. The resulting baked fruit stays very moist, and doesn't need any additional liquid, which can water down the natural flavor of the fruit. But it also doesn't dehydrate, so the outcome is a cross between a compote and traditional baked fruit. I have a trick to bridge the difference: I bake two kinds of fruit together. One I cut into small pieces (which becomes the compote) and the other I leave whole or in halves, and stuff much as I would oven-bake fruit. The result here is a combination of moist, sweet, slightly al dente pears in a chunky spiced applesauce. Serve it warm with shortbread or chocolate cookies, or with ice cream.

6

SERVINGS

PRECOOK

15 minutes

SLOW COOK

3 to 4 hours on high
in a 5- to 6-quart
slow cooker

1	cup raisins	½	lemon, juiced
½	cup light brown sugar	3	firm pears, such as Bosc
½	teaspoon ground cinnamon	2	crisp apples, such as Granny Smith
2	tablespoons unsalted butter, melted	1	teaspoon vanilla extract

MIX the raisins, brown sugar, cinnamon, and butter together in a small bowl; set aside.

PEEL the zest from the lemon in strips with a vegetable peeler; scatter over the bottom of a 5- to 6-quart slow cooker.

PUT the lemon juice into a medium mixing bowl. Peel the pears and apples, tossing them in the lemon juice as they are peeled. Cut the fruit in half from stem to bottom and scoop out the cores with a melon baller. Cut each apple half into 6 chunks, coating the cut surfaces with lemon juice as they are cut, and scatter on top of the lemon strips.

PLACE the pears, hollow sides up, on top of the apples, and fill each hollow with a portion of the raisin mixture; scatter the remaining raisin mixture over the fruit. Drizzle the vanilla over the fruit. Cover the cooker with a folded dish towel and top with a lid. Cook on high for 3 to 4 hours, until the fruit is soft and the liquid is bubbling around the edges. Keep warm for up to 2 hours, and serve warm.

what else?

- This recipe is just as good if you cut the pears into chunks and leave the apples in halves.

- Feel free to replace the lemon juice with lime or orange juice.

Sweet Potato Pumpkin Pudding

In the Caribbean, sweet potato and pumpkin are used interchangeably in puddings and pies. Heavily spiced and creamed with condensed milk or coconut milk, they are the definition of homemade comfort food. This simple pudding can be assembled in minutes and left to steam all day in a slow cooker. Utterly delicious (I have trouble refraining from eating it raw), it is one of the few desserts that will deliver a portion of vegetables while it tames your sweet tooth.

8-10

SERVINGS

PRECOOK

5 minutes

SLOW COOK

6 to 8 hours on low in a 1-quart ovenproof mixing bowl or pudding mold set into a 3½-quart, or larger, slow cooker

AT THE END

30 minutes cooling

1   can (about 15 ounces) sweet potatoes in syrup, drained

1   can (about 15 ounces) 100% pure pumpkin

¼   teaspoon ground cinnamon

¼   teaspoon ground ginger

¼   teaspoon ground aniseed

      Pinch of ground cloves

2   large or extra-large eggs

½   cup canned coconut milk (not light)

½   cup granulated sugar

½   cup light brown sugar

½   teaspoon kosher salt

2   tablespoon flour

2   tablespoons unsalted butter, melted

COMBINE all the ingredients in a food processor and purée until smooth. Pour into a 1-quart ovenproof mixing bowl or pudding mold, cover with foil, and tie in place with string. Place inside a 3½-quart, or larger, slow cooker and pour boiling water into the crock so that it comes about 1 inch up the sides of the bowl. Cover the cooker and cook on low for 6 to 8 hours, or until a tester inserted in the center comes out clean.

COOL for at least 30 minutes, and serve warm, at room temperature, or chilled.

what else?

- You can substitute cooked sweet potatoes and any squash with orange flesh, such as butternut or acorn, for the canned ingredients.

- Reduced-fat coconut milk will tend to curdle in this recipe; avoid it.

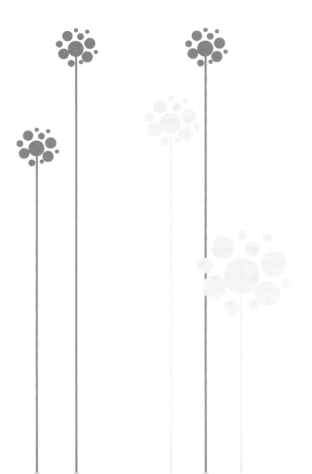

Caramelized Brown Betty

Let's get this straight. A "crisp" is a layer of sweetened and spiced fruit baked under a crispy crumb topping; a "pandowdy" is a one-crust, deep-dish fruit pie with a biscuit topping; and a "betty" (or "Brown Betty") is a pudding made with fruit, layered and topped with buttered breadcrumbs. Although they are all good, Betty is my queen. I've messed with the original a little by using bread cubes instead of crumbs, which gives the finished pudding a bit more texture.

3   tablespoons unsalted butter, plus
    3 tablespoons, melted

6   firm Bosc pears or Granny Smith apples or
    large ripe peaches, peeled, cored, and
    cut into 1-inch dice

1   cup firmly packed light brown sugar

1   teaspoon vanilla extract

3   cups cubed fresh or day-old bread
    (¼-inch cubes)

¼   teaspoon ground cinnamon

6–8

SERVINGS

PRECOOK

10 minutes

SLOW COOK

3 hours on high
in a 3- to 4-quart
cooker

MELT the 3 tablespoons of solid butter in a large skillet over high heat until foamy. Add the fruit and sauté until the pieces just begin to brown, about 5 minutes. Remove from the heat and mix in the brown sugar and vanilla.

MIX the 3 tablespoons of melted butter and the bread cubes in a medium bowl until the butter coats the bread evenly. Scatter a third of the bread over the bottom of a 3- to 4-quart slow cooker. Top with half the fruit mixture, another third of the bread, the remaining fruit, and the remaining bread. Sprinkle the cinnamon over the top. Drape a folded kitchen towel over the top and cover with the lid. Cook for 3 hours on high, or until the fruit is bubbling and brown around the edges.

KEEP WARM for up to 2 hours and serve warm with ice cream, if desired.

Arborio Rice Pudding
with Tart Cherries and Mint

Rice is disastrous in a slow cooker. It gets mushy, broken, sticky, and sodden. But rice pudding—that's another matter. In fact, the very deficiencies of slow-cooked rice turn into assets in a pudding. Although it can be made with any rice, I find that a medium- or short-grained rice, like Arborio, gives the creamiest results. This pudding is perfumed exotically with fresh mint and sour cherries.

1	teaspoon unsalted butter		¼	cup finely chopped fresh mint
½	cup Arborio rice, rinsed		2	large eggs
⅓	cup (2 ounces) dried sour cherries			Pinch of salt
2	cups whole milk		1½	teaspoons vanilla extract
2	cups half-and-half		⅛	teaspoon almond extract
¾	cup sugar, divided			

6–8

SERVINGS

PRECOOK

10 minutes

SLOW COOK

4 hours on high in a 1½-quart soufflé dish set into a 6-quart, or larger, slow cooke

AT THE END

1 hour cooling

BUTTER the interior of a 1½-quart soufflé dish with a diameter of 6½ inches or less. Add the rice and cherries and set aside.

HEAT the milk, half-and-half, ½ cup of the sugar, and the mint in a medium saucepan over medium heat until bubbles form around the edges of the milk, about 5 minutes. Set aside to steep for 2 minutes, and strain.

MEANWHILE, beat the eggs, the remaining ¼ cup sugar, the salt, vanilla, and almond extract in a medium mixing bowl until well combined.

SLOWLY POUR a third of the hot milk mixture into the eggs, stirring constantly. Continue to add the milk in thirds, stirring until everything is well blended. Pour into the soufflé dish and stir until the rice and cherries are moistened.

COVER the top with heavy-duty foil and crimp the edges tightly. Place inside a 6-quart, or larger, slow cooker and pour enough boiling water into the crock around the soufflé dish to reach 1 inch up the sides of the soufflé dish. Cover the cooker and cook for 4 hours on high, or until the custard is set across the top. You will not be able to see any rice on the surface. Remove the pudding from the cooker and cool until barely warm, about 1 hour.

WHEN COOL, stir the pudding with a fork, incorporating the creamy custard on the top with the more solid rice on the bottom. Serve immediately or store, tightly covered, in a refrigerator for up to 2 days. Serve at room temperature or chilled.

what else?

- If you prefer your rice pudding with more distinct rice grains, use long-grain rice rather than Arborio. The proportions can remain the same.

- If you are feeling a bit adventurous, replace the mint with fresh basil. The combination of cherries and basil is remarkable, very floral, with a subtle scent of anise.

- Or, if you like your rice pudding more traditional, just substitute golden raisins for cherries and 1 teaspoon ground cinnamon for the mint. Keep everything else the same.

Ricotta Vanilla Bread Pudding

If food were a substitute for sex, you would be fortunate to experience anything as erotic as this luxurious dessert. A pillow-soft cross between cheesecake and bread pudding, delicately scented with floral vanilla and as light as it is rich, it overwhelms the senses with each bite. In fact, to be honest, I usually don't waste it on dessert, where it has to compete with dinner for attention. I prefer it for breakfast or as the star of a special brunch. Many years ago I served it for brunch on New Year's Day. It was an exceptional year.

2	tablespoons unsalted butter, melted, divided
4	slices white bread, raisin bread, challah, or other egg bread, cut into ½-inch cubes
½	cup golden raisins
1	cup whole milk
1	container (about 15 ounces) whole-milk ricotta cheese
½	cup sugar
2	large eggs
1	cup sour cream
1	teaspoon finely grated lemon zest
1	teaspoon vanilla extract
¼	teaspoon ground cinnamon

6-8

SERVINGS

PRECOOK

15 minutes

SLOW COOK

2 to 3 hours on high in a 1½-quart soufflé dish set into a 6-quart, or larger, slow cooker

AT THE END

4 to 5 minutes

COAT a 1½-quart soufflé dish with half the butter. Toss the bread and raisins together in the prepared dish. Pour the milk over them and toss again lightly until the bread is completely moistened; set aside for 10 minutes.

MEANWHILE, mix the ricotta cheese, sugar, eggs, sour cream, lemon zest, and vanilla in a large mixing bowl. Pour over the bread and raisins and mix lightly. Drizzle the remaining butter over the top and sprinkle with the cinnamon. Cover the top with heavy-duty aluminum foil and crimp the edges securely. Place in the slow cooker and pour enough boiling water into the crock around the soufflé dish to reach 1 inch up the sides. Cover the top of the cooker with a folded kitchen towel and top with the lid. Cook for 2 to 3 hours on high, or until a tester inserted in the center comes out with just a few specks clinging to it. Remove the pudding from the cooker and cool for at least 20 minutes or to room temperature.

MEANWHILE, preheat a broiler. Place the pudding under the broiler about 6 inches from the heat and broil until the top browns lightly, 4 to 5 minutes. Serve warm or at room temperature.

what else?

- Serve with warm Chunky Applesauce (page 188) or vanilla pear sauce (see What Else?, page 189), if desired.

Supremely Edible Fruitcake

Fruitcake-phobes take heed: you can stop your sniggering and drop the jokes. I offer this extravagance to banish the fruitcake's doorstop image forever. Chock full of nuts and dried fruit (none of those cloying candied citron bits), doused in brandy, and drizzled with brandy glaze, the cake is as opulent as it is delicious. But the real wonder is that it is baked in a slow cooker—a revelation. Like all fruit-cakes, it will keep in the refrigerator, tightly wrapped, for months, and, okay, it makes a great doorstop.

1	pound walnut halves or pecan halves
1	pound dried fruit (a mixture of apricots, figs, prunes, and/or dates), cut into quarters
1	cup golden raisins
¾	cup flour
½	teaspoon baking powder
¼	teaspoon salt
1	cup sugar

3	large eggs, lightly beaten
1	teaspoon vanilla extract
	Nonstick oil spray
¼	cup to 6 tablespoons brandy (depending on whether you make icing)
¾	cup confectioners' sugar (optional)
2	tablespoons melted unsalted butter (optional)

MIX the nuts, mixed dried fruit, and raisins in a large mixing bowl.

MIX the flour, baking powder, salt, and sugar in a medium bowl. Toss 3 tablespoons of the flour mixture with the nuts and fruit. Add the eggs and vanilla to the remaining flour mixture and beat to form a smooth batter. Scrape into the bowl with the nuts and fruit and toss with a rubber spatula until the nuts and fruit are well coated with batter.

SPRAY the interior of a 1½-quart soufflé dish with oil. Scrape the batter-coated nuts and fruit into the dish, wet your hands with cold water, and pack the nuts and fruit firmly into the dish. Set in a 6-quart, or larger, slow cooker, cover the cooker with a folded kitchen towel, and place the lid on top. Cook on low for 6 hours, or until a skewer inserted in the center comes out clean.

REMOVE the dish from the cooker and spoon ¼ cup of the brandy over the top. Cool on a rack for 30 minutes. Run a knife around the edges of the cake to loosen, invert onto a rack, and remove the soufflé dish. Turn the cake right-side up and cool to room temperature.

CONTINUED

12

SERVINGS

PRECOOK

15 minutes

SLOW COOK

6 hours on high in a 1½-quart soufflé dish set into a 6-quart, or larger, slow cooker

AT THE END

2 hours cooling

Supremely Edible Fruitcake CONTINUED

IF YOU LIKE, you can drizzle the cake with icing: Mix the confectioners' sugar, melted butter, and remaining 2 tablespoons brandy with a whisk until smooth. Drizzle over the top of the cake.

what else?

- If you don't have a slow cooker with a timer and you need to be away for more than 6 hours, you can lengthen the cooking time of this cake to 8 hours by mixing the batter ahead of time, packing it into the soufflé dish, and chilling it for several hours. Because it contains a significant amount of sugar and very little protein, there is no food safety danger.

- Change the liquor to suit your taste. The cake is delicious doused with amaretto, Frangelico, Nocello, or any other nut-flavored liqueur.

- For chocolate fruitcake, replace 1 tablespoon flour with 2 tablespoons Dutch-process unsweetened cocoa powder.

Brandied Fruit

You will never be caught short for an elegant dessert if you have some brandied fruit stowed away. It takes minutes to assemble, offers complete relaxation during cooking, and will remain aromatic and sweet well into the next life, if stored, tightly closed, in a refrigerator. In this recipe I have used a combination of figs, apricots, and prunes, but you can use the same weight of any dried fruit. Serve it chilled or warmed with ice cream, cake, or cookies, and if you don't mind a little nip upon waking, it's not a bad start to the day.

8	ounces dried Calimyrna figs	⅔	cup boiling water
12	ounces dried apricot halves	2	cinnamon sticks
1	pound pitted prunes	2	whole cloves
	Finely julienned zest and juice of 1 lemon	1	vanilla bean, split
	Finely julienned zest and juice of 1 orange	1	cup brandy
⅔	cup honey		

LAYER the fruit in a 3½- to 5-quart slow cooker, figs first, then apricots, and then prunes. Scatter the lemon and orange zest over the top, and drizzle the lemon and orange juice over all. Dissolve the honey in the boiling water and pour over the fruit. Imbed the cinnamon, cloves, and vanilla bean in the fruit. Cook on high for 3 to 4 hours, until all of the fruit is soft. Remove from the heat and pour the brandy over all; let rest for 24 hours at room temperature before serving.

REMOVE the cinnamon sticks, cloves, and vanilla bean pod. Serve with ice cream, cookies, or cake, if desired.

6-8

SERVINGS

PRECOOK
5 minutes

SLOW COOK
3 to 4 hours on high in a 3½- to 5-quart slow cooker

AT THE END
24 hours resting

Slow-Cooked Brandy Cheesecake

A cheesecake is nothing more than a custard in which cream cheese takes the place of milk. Like all custards, it needs to cook gently, just the thing for a slow cooker. Think about it. Cheesecake is typically baked in a pan of water set in a 350°F oven. The reason for the water is to keep the temperature next to the cake below 212°F (the temperature of boiling water at sea level), so that the edge of the filling never gets much hotter than its coagulation point (around 180°F). Since the average temperature of a slow cooker set on low is 200°F, slow-cooked cheese cake comes out completely creamy from edge to edge. This cheesecake is seductively pure and rich, flavored with nothing more than a dram of brandy and a whisper of vanilla.

Nonstick oil spray

¼ **cup graham cracker crumbs or other cookie crumbs**

1½ **pounds cream cheese, regular or lite (not fat-free), at room temperature**

¾ **cup sugar**

1 **tablespoon vanilla extract**

3 **tablespoons brandy**

4 **extra-large eggs**

SPRAY the inside of a 1½-quart soufflé dish with oil and dust the sides and bottom with the crumbs; set aside.

BEAT the cream cheese, sugar, vanilla, and brandy in a large mixing bowl, by hand or with an electric mixer, until well combined, scraping down the bowl as necessary. Add the eggs, beating just until incorporated into the batter.

POUR the batter into the prepared soufflé dish. Cut a round of parchment paper or wax paper just large enough to fit the top. Spray with oil and place, oil side down, on top of the batter. Cover the dish with a sheet of heavy aluminum foil, crimping the edges to secure it tightly. Set the soufflé dish on a long sheet of foil and wrap it over the top, completely enclosing the dish in foil. Place the dish in the center of a 6-quart, or larger, slow cooker. Pour boiling water into the cooker so it comes 1½ inches up the sides of the dish. Cover the cooker and cook for 8 to 10 hours on low, until set in the center.

REMOVE the dish and unwrap; place on a rack and cool to room temperature, about 1 hour. Cover with plastic, invert onto a plate, and remove the soufflé dish. Invert onto a serving plate and refrigerate for at least 3 hours, or for up to 3 days.

WHEN READY TO SERVE, cut the cheesecake into wedges with a knife with a thin blade, dipping it in water between cuts.

12

SERVINGS

PRECOOK
15 minutes

SLOW COOK
8 to 10 hours on low in a 1½-quart soufflé dish set into a 6-quart, or larger, slow cooker

AT THE END
4 hours cooling

Chocolate-Covered Coconut Torte

This super-sized chocolate and coconut patty looks like a cake and bakes like a cake, but all it takes is one bite to know that it's more of a candy than a baked good. It has no flour (a boon for the gluten-intolerant) and no leavener. It neither rises nor falls. Rather, the ingredients meld into the richest, dampest, most flavor-sodden confection you are likely to pull from the inner reaches of your slow cooker. You can slow-cook the torte days ahead of serving (it will keep flawlessly, tightly wrapped in the refrigerator, for up to a week) and glaze it no more than a day ahead. Because it has no flour, it will never go stale and will stay fresh-tasting for days, if it lasts that long. Serve in small wedges; a little goes a long way.

SERVINGS

PRECOOK

15 minutes

SLOW COOK

2 to 3 hours on high in a 1½-quart soufflé dish or 6-inch cheesecake pan set into a 6-quart, or larger, slow cooker

AT THE END

20 minutes plus 1 hour cooling

---

8 tablespoons (1 stick) unsalted butter, divided

4 ounces white chocolate, chopped, or ½ cup white chocolate chips

Pinch of salt

1 teaspoon vanilla extract

3 cups (12 ounces) sweetened shredded coconut

¾ cup confectioners' sugar

3 large eggs, lightly beaten

Nonstick oil spray

1 ounce semi-sweet chocolate, chopped

1 ounce unsweetened chocolate, chopped

1 teaspoon honey

COMBINE 6 tablespoons of the butter and the white chocolate in a large microwave-safe bowl, cover, and cook in a microwave at full power until half melted, about 1 minute. Remove the cover and whisk until the chocolate is completely melted.

STIR in the salt, vanilla, coconut, and confectioners' sugar and mix until well combined. Add the eggs, beating until well incorporated into the batter.

SPRAY a 1½-quart soufflé dish 6½ inches in diameter or less, or a 6-inch cheesecake pan, with oil and line the bottom with a circle of parchment or foil. Spray the lining with oil. Scrape the batter into the pan and press down to pack firmly. Cover the dish with a sheet of heavy-duty aluminum foil, crimping the edges to secure it tightly, and place in a 6-quart, or larger, slow cooker. Pour enough boiling water into the crock surrounding the cake pan to come 1½ inches up the sides. Cover the cooker and cook on high for 2 to 3 hours, until a cake tester inserted in the center comes out almost clean.

REMOVE the foil and cool the torte in the pan on a rack for 30 minutes. Run a knife around the edges of the torte and unmold onto a plate. Remove the paper liner from the cake. Cool to room temperature on a rack.

MEANWHILE, make the icing: Put the remaining 2 tablespoons butter, the two types of dark chocolate, and the honey in a medium microwave-safe bowl. Cover and cook in a microwave at full power until half melted, about 45 seconds. Remove the cover and stir to combine. Let rest until the chocolate has thickened enough to coat a spoon, about 30 minutes.

TO ICE THE TORTE, set the cake, still on the rack, over a drip pan. Pour half the glaze over top, and smooth it over the top and around the sides with an icing spatula with a flat blade. Pour the rest over the top and smooth the top. With a large, wide spatula, transfer the cake to a serving plate. Allow to rest until the glaze sets, about 30 minutes.

Candied Clementine and Kalamata Compote

I love this stuff. It was the first thing I ever made in a slow cooker, and I continue to stock my pantry with it every year when clementines come into season. The combination of bittersweet fruit and salty olives is mindblowing on multiple levels. On the palate it's an education, as every taste bud in your mouth fires simultaneously. It's creamy with a minimum of fat, aromatic without a trace of herb, and completely addictive (only shame will keep you from consuming the entire batch in a single sitting). I usually serve it with toast at breakfast, but I've also been known to go at it with a spoon late at night.

1	cup sugar	2	tablespoons orange liqueur
10	clementines, cut into ¼-inch-thick slices	24	pitted kalamata olives, coarsely chopped

SCATTER ⅓ cup of the sugar over the bottom of a 3- to 4-quart slow cooker. Layer the clementine slices over the sugar, and scatter the remaining ⅔ cup sugar over the top. Cover the crock with a folded kitchen towel, cover with the lid, and cook on high for 4 hours, or until the fruit is soft and a syrup has formed in the bottom of the crock.

UNCOVER, and drizzle the liqueur over the top. Cool the compote and mix in the olives. Serve as a topping with toast or sweet rolls.

8

SERVINGS
(2 cups)

PRECOOK
10 minutes

SLOW COOK
4 hours on high
in a 3- to 4-quart
slow cooker

AT THE END
5 minutes plus
1 hour cooling

Warm Bar

Before the advent of ice makers and central heating, warm party drinks were the rule. Mulled wines, spiced cider, hot buttered rum, and mead have all but disappeared, but your slow cooker can reinstate their renown. The "warm" setting on a slow cooker holds drinks at a perfect sipping temperature, keeping any alcohol in the recipe just at the point of vaporizing, a fleeting moment when the aromas are at their height. Warm drinks come in two styles: spiced and sweetened. The Mulled Wine and Spiced Cider recipes that follow are of the spiced school, in which everything is combined and heated. The Hot Buttered Rum and Modern-Day Mead recipes call for creating a sweet liquid in the cooker before you add the booze.

12
SERVINGS

PRECOOK
3 minutes

SLOW COOK
2 to 4 hours on low, and up to 6 hours on warm while serving, in a 4-quart slow cooker

FOR MULLED WINE

3	quarts fruity red wine, such as Shiraz, Merlot, or Cabernet
12	pitted dates, chopped
12	dried apricots, chopped
½	cup raisins
	Finely grated zest of 1 orange
1	cinnamon stick, about 2 inches
1	slice gingerroot, about ½ inch thick
2	whole cloves
⅛	teaspoon ground nutmeg

FOR SPICED CIDER

3	quarts unsweetened apple cider
12	dried apple slices, chopped
	Finely grated zest of 1 lemon
1	cinnamon stick, about 2 inches
2	slices gingerroot, about ½ inch thick
2	whole cloves
⅛	teaspoon ground nutmeg

FOR HOT BUTTERED RUM

6	cups water
1½	cups light brown sugar
1	vanilla bean, split
6	cups dark rum
4	tablespoons unsalted butter, cut into 12 pieces

FOR MODERN-DAY MEAD

6	cups water
2	cups honey
4	cups brandy

TO MAKE THE MULLED WINE OR SPICED CIDER, combine all ingredients in a 4-quart slow cooker. Cover the cooker and cook for 3 to 4 hours on low; keep warm while serving. Try to avoid serving any of the whole spices.

TO MAKE HOT BUTTERED RUM, combine the water, brown sugar, and vanilla bean in a 4-quart slow cooker; cover the cooker and cook for 2 to 3 hours on low. Add the rum and cook for another hour; keep warm while serving. Add a piece of butter to each portion as you serve. Do not serve the vanilla bean.

TO MAKE MODERN-DAY MEAD, combine the water and honey in a 4-quart slow cooker; cover the cooker and cook for 2 to 3 hours on low. Add the brandy and cook for another hour; keep warm while serving.

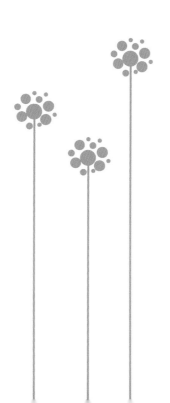

Index

Index

table of equivalents

The exact equivalents in the following tables have been rounded for convenience.

LIQUID/DRY MEASUREMENTS

U.S.	METRIC
¼ teaspoon	1.25 milliliters
½ teaspoon	2.5 milliliters
1 teaspoon	5 milliliters
1 tablespoon (3 teaspoons)	15 milliliters
1 fluid ounce (2 tablespoons)	30 milliliters
¼ cup	60 milliliters
⅓ cup	80 milliliters
½ cup	120 milliliters
1 cup	240 milliliters
1 pint (2 cups)	480 milliliters
1 quart (4 cups, 32 ounces)	960 milliliters
1 gallon (4 quarts)	3.84 liters
1 ounce (by weight)	28 grams
1 pound	448 grams
2.2 pounds	1 kilogram

LENGTHS

U.S.	METRIC
⅛ inch	3 millimeters
¼ inch	6 millimeters
½ inch	12 millimeters
1 inch	2.5 centimeters

OVEN TEMPERATURES

FAHRENHEIT	CELSIUS	GAS
250	120	½
275	140	1
300	150	2
325	160	3
350	180	4
375	190	5
400	200	6
425	220	7
450	230	8
475	240	9
500	260	10